#Jesus

#Jesus

Wow...Trusting God Works!

Robert L. Bostic

#Jesus: Wow... Trusting God Works!
by Robert L. Bostic

Cover Design by Atinad Designs.

© Copyright 2014

SAINT PAUL PRESS, DALLAS, TEXAS

First Printing, 2014

All rights reserved. No part of this publication may be reproduced, stored in a retrieval system, or transmitted in any form or by any means, electronic, mechanical, photocopying, recording, or otherwise, without the prior permission of the copyright owner, except for brief quotations included in a review of the book.

All scripture quotations, unless otherwise listed, are taken from the Thompson Chain Reference Study Bible (King James Version).

ISBN-10: 0-9915856-8-2
ISBN-13: 978-0-9915856-8-7

Printed in the U.S.A.

We are excited you have chosen to read this book, and we are anxious to hear from you concerning your thoughts, opinions, suggestions, or any comments you may have about your experiences. It is the author's hope that all who read this book will find encouragement from the experiences he faced and how he worked through the seasons and storms of life—seasons and storms that are common to everyone. Please send your input to Robert.bostic@yahoo.com.

Foreword

"Fail to plan, plan to fail" is an expression I heard at an early age and have applied it often throughout my career. Developing and starting with a plan is where I am the most comfortable. Often the plan must be adjusted as unforeseen circumstances arise but I simply respond to each event, based on my knowledge and experience. When creating the plan, I always have the end in mind and my focus is on constructing the most effective strategy to reach my goal.

I have older siblings that I have watched during the course of my life and have gained knowledge from their experiences. I paid close attention to their successes and failures and learned from both. There were joys that I experienced because I recalled things that brought them happiness. There were heartaches that I was able to better handle because I remembered how they responded to these undesirable situations. This has sometimes given me a slight advantage in dealing with significant moments in life.

When reading this book, I encourage you to adopt the author as an older sibling. Listen and put to memory, the stories he tells. As you walk this journey with him, pay close attention to how he obtained joy. Learn from the heartaches he experienced and how he responded to each situation. Most importantly, notice the one thing that is consistent throughout the book. There is a specific friend that was always there for him and the author mentions his name repeatedly throughout his writings. You will also notice that the author refers to excerpts from the ultimate book of plans, which was written with the end in mind.

I attended a festival, in my home town several years ago and this particular event was highlighting talent from many of the local churches. Being a Worship Leader, I was drawn in quickly by the music, being blessed, listening for new material and what other churches were doing with their congregations. I clearly remember something else catching my attention. The Master of Ceremonies was equipped with a special ability to communicate and an obvious passion for Jesus. His voice was unique and gentle, yet that of a leader. It was sometimes filled with emotion but quick to recover as he drove the message home with confidence. There was something different about this man.

Since that evening in 1985, I have witnessed God do some amazing things through this man and was excited when he decided to write about Jesus and how He is and has been the Provider, the Healer, the Prince of Peace, the Victor and Friend.

The author, Mr. Robert (Bob) Bostic is an ordinary guy whom God has used to do some extraordinary things. Be blessed and encouraged as you take this journey with him. I urge you to look at each chapter as a stop along the road. You may have already traveled some of these roads but this time, I am confident that you will notice new places of interest. Perhaps one day, you may want to return to some of the roadside stops, as you journey through your own life. Most importantly, you will notice who Bob's constant travel companion has been. You see, this companion has already been there, He knows the road well and you can trust Him.

"The book, #Jesus, was for me, as temperature is to a thermometer, as water is to dry ground, as notes are to a song and as hope is to the hopeless. If you want to be better equipped to find hope in life, travel this journey with the author. #Jesus is an authentic account of how loss can be turned to gain and sorrow can be replaced with joy. #Jesus will be my go-to-book for years to come as this powerful book of great inspiration, hope and encouragement speaks truth, offers hope and brings renewed relevance to scripture."

Brian Poling, Worship Leader
First Baptist Church, Greensburg, Indiana

Who is Bob Bostic?

God has poured so many blessings into my life that, unless I 'unload,' I am going to explode; hence, the writing of this book. It could be best explained as being like a heart with a defective aortic valve, thus preventing the blood from flowing back into the left ventricle of the heart, therefore, death could occur from the heart exploding in a massive heart attack at any moment due to the build up of blood in the heart.

My aortic valve of blessings is the body, mind, and spirit that God has filled to the point of satisfaction and contentment and the need to share my story in hopes that others might discover the similarities between our lives and be encouraged or motivated to accept their daily lives as an opportunity to move forward despite circumstances or situations that might attempt to discourage them in life.

I am much like the man, Agur, of the Holy Bible in Proverbs 30:7-9, where I pleaded with God to provide me with "just enough" to live a satisfied life. Agur said specifically in verse 8, "Give me neither poverty nor riches; feed me with food convenient for me." He explained his request for "just enough" in verse 9, saying, "Lest I be full, and deny thee, and say, Who is the Lord? Or lest I be poor, and steal, and take the name of my God in vain."

Yes, "just enough" has been an on-going theme in my life as God has proven that He will add physical blessings as an extension of His spiritual blessings to anyone who lives a life of obedience to Him.

I would not have chosen my life's path, but as I look back, it is evident God has had His hands continually on my back guiding me, and His arms tightly around me comforting and sustaining me when disappointments, confusion, barricades, detours, or interruptions happened.

My parents, my brothers, and my relatives have all been "pillars" of strength in helping to shape my life. My immediate family and all my friends have shown unconditional love in supporting my development.

I accepted Christ into my heart at thirteen years of age, was baptized on April 1, 1956, and at age twenty-one felt the hands of God on my back during the singing of an invitational hymn at the conclusion of a small country church revival. I found myself standing at the altar of the church weeping and telling the pastor that although I did not know what I truly wanted to do, I knew I wanted to commit to "doing whatever God wanted me to do in the future."

As a young married man with a wife and two daughters, and growing in a culture limited in its knowledge of knowing all God might want a person to do in a lifetime, it was natural for me to think God was "calling" me to go into full-time ministry preaching and teaching His Word.

I struggled daily between "answering the call" and getting my family through financial difficulties. I could never feel comfortable "giving it all up" and began to look for ways to "serve God" while continuing to meet my family obligations.

My spiritual search for serving God was revealed to me during a Bible study with a group of men discussing a session on "Gifts" from the study guide of, *If You Want to Walk on Water, You've Got to Get Out of the Boat*, written by John Ortberg, senior pastor at Menlo Park Presbyterian Church in Menlo Park, California, and previously a teaching pastor at Willow Creek Community Church. The chapters point out many "gifts" given by God that people often "bury" or "hide away" because of fear or misunderstanding, and therefore miss out on the spiritual reward of seeing God honor their life of obedience.

The men's discussion flipped a switch in my mind that allowed me to see that I had misunderstood that country church revival altar call way back in 1963. I realized I had been feeling guilty for not going into the "professional" ministry and becoming a church pastor. God was calling me to a ministry to serve Him as a son, a brother, a husband, a father, a relative, a friend, a co-worker, a youth leader/sponsor, a Bible study teacher, and a person who found success in my vocational occupations. I realized that God's gift to me was to use my abilities in all areas of life giving Him the glory while seeking "just enough" to provide financially for my family.

I am thankful that I was daily motivated to live for Jesus despite my personal guilt from not going into the professional pastoral ministry. Now I understand why God rewarded me so faithfully along the way. I have been using the "gift" God provided me with—that "touch on my back," being pushed down that church aisle to the altar—by getting out of my lifeboat, and working each job as though I was doing it for the Lord. I am thankful that although I did not fully understand, I trusted God and began living a life as described in I Peter 4:11: "If any man speak, let him speak as the oracles of God; if any man minister, let him do it as of the ability which God giveth; that God in all things may be glorified through Jesus Christ, to whom be praise and dominion for ever and ever. Amen."

My life is nothing special. My life has been blessed and, along the way, I have grown content in all that I have. Although I do not compare my pleasure and satisfaction with fame and fortune, I am quick to suggest that living a life devoted to telling others about Jesus in our homes, on our jobs, to our friends, in our communities, and in our personal lives will deliver the riches of glory through the grace of God.

I have been given much, have had much taken away, and I live today proclaiming a life filled with happiness found in love, joy, peace, longsuffering, gentleness, goodness, faith, meekness, and temperance of the Christian "fruits of the spirit" (Galatians 5:22-23).

I love Jesus, talk of Jesus, and in this book, I relate how trusting Jesus provides a life worth living! Maybe one particular chapter will relate to your life, and maybe after reading all of them, you will discover God can lead you through anything that could possibly interrupt your peace and joy!

Contents

Prologue: #Jesus…Thank You 19
Chapter 1: #Jesus… Are You There? 23
Chapter 2: #Jesus… What Is It All About? 27
Chapter 3: #Jesus… He Never Changes! 31
Chapter 4: #Jesus…Where Is God? 39
Chapter 5: #Jesus … Is It Worth the Effort? 51
Chapter 6: #Jesus… God Is Real 55
Chapter 7: #Jesus… Seek God, Find God 67
Chapter 8: #Jesus … Marriage Till Death
 Do Us Part 71
Chapter 9: #Jesus … Extraordinary Things 83
Chapter 10: #Jesus… Jobs 89
Chapter 11: #Jesus…Today, Tomorrow,
 & Forever..97
Chapter 12: #Jesus… Friends 103
Chapter 13: #Jesus… Disappointments 111
Chapter 14: #Jesus… Eternal Happiness 117
Chapter 15:#Jesus… He Provides 121
Chapter 16: #Jesus… Retirement 125
Chapter 17: #Jesus… Simply Trust 135
Chapter 18: #Jesus… Barrel Life,
 Good Example..139
Chapter 19: #Jesus…The First Shall Be Last 151
Chapter 20: #Jesus… Gifts From God 155
Chapter 21: #Jesus… 27 Reasons To Trust 165
Chapter 22: #Jesus… Steps to Trusting God 169

Prologue
#Jesus... Thank You

Thank You, God, for giving to me, thy great salvation so rich and free! Those are a few words of a Christian hymn I learned while being dragged to church with my loving mom and dad at a time when the music alone seemed to be the traditional thing to do in church.

Little did I know that God would honor my mom and dad and deliver His biblical promise that, if you train up a child in the way he should go, when he is old he will not depart from it (Proverbs 22:6). Unknown to me, I was developing Christian habits that appeared very normal and non-threatening as obedience to the discipline of loving parents became a daily way of life that shaped my future no matter how I felt about it at the time.

Overlooking my childhood tantrums, fits, rebellion, and rudeness, my parents loved me enough to suffer embarrassment and finger pointing while taking me in and out of church every time the doors opened; they never yielded to my begging and pleading to let me stay home!

Thank goodness they persisted, because life has been tough enough attempting to follow in their footsteps by striving to live a life for Jesus to the point where I can't imagine how bad things would be if God wasn't leading and comforting me and if He really did not exist! Proverbs 3:5-6 have become biblical truths that drive my daily walk in God's words to "trust in the Lord with all your heart, and lean not on your own understanding; in all your way acknowledge him, and he shall direct your paths."

Thank you, Mom and Dad, and may you be singing in the Heavenly Choir for our Lord as I write these memories in hopes that I, too, will again be following your lead and, perhaps, be invited to sing alongside you one day soon. I have through your example and your encouragement, accepted in my heart God's gift of love: "For God so loved the world that he gave his only begotten son that whosoever believes in him should not perish but have everlasting life" (John 3:16).

Thank you, Mom and Dad, for giving me guidelines to live by, and for trusting me in the process while knowing many times I would fall short of the glory of God (Romans 3:23) as well as your family standards. Your allowing me to learn my way through survival with three other brothers in our home, your protective hand in rescuing me when needed, and your praise of small victories in my quest gave me a glimpse as to how love is really expressed within our hearts through the quality of life only a family can provide.

Thank you, Mom and Dad, for slipping me a little change, for always making my birthdays special, and although hidden to my eyes, for sacrificing your portion of the necessities needed so that I might not want (Psalm 23). Your love exemplified God's promise that He would never leave us nor forsake us (Hebrews 13:5), and He would supply all my needs (Philippians 4:19).

Thank you, Mom and Dad, for rewarding me for good choices with freedom to grow and explore and for discipline when I made wrong choices to bring me back to the reality of the need to live on the straight and narrow way (Matthew 7:13-14). Your unconditional love taught me trust through obedience and gave me confidence to succeed as promised in 1 John 4:7-11.

Thank you, Mom and Dad, for giving to me your great love so rich and free! Thank you for making the words of that old favorite hymn come alive in my life. I know you are receiving the biblical fruits of Ephesians 6:8 as your heavenly reward. Your parental guidance and example have me looking forward to one day also hearing those greeting words, "Well done, thou good and faithful servant" (Matthew 25:21).

Wow!

CHAPTER 1
#Jesus... Are You There?

If God is always there, why can't we find Him? We live in a world that provides information instantly at the stroke of a keypad, iPad screen, keyboard, or from speaking commands into a voice-sensitive device. However, many never see the unconditional love God offers, and therefore, struggle aimlessly attempting to find an answer to the challenging question, "God, are You there?"

Society has clouded the issue of the existence of God by allowing freedom of speech to everyone in America whereby citizens can express their own personal belief or denial in one God. This has resulted in an unclear explanation of just who God is and an unsatisfactory answer to the question, "God, are You there?" The United States of America, in my opinion, is the greatest country in the world, offering its citizens the freedom to think without restraint. The freedom to choose is probably one of the strongest attraction points of people wanting to live in the USA. Yet, people who claim their belief in a God who offers eternal life through believing by faith in the existence of God's Son, Jesus, are increasingly being limited in their freedom to express their belief, and therefore, limited as to its teachings.

Society is unable to physically stand and unequivocally point to one God who is acceptable to all citizens of America. There is no God that can be interviewed or photographed on the world wide web, the giant network television stations, or powerful cable companies found by satellite circling the globe, or be quoted daily in press releases through the respected newspapers or magazines of the world. Finding God requires personal effort and is left solely up to each individual.

The answer requires each person to experience a personal relationship with the understanding that what just got them through a difficult situation was something which occurred totally out of their control.

I suggest that you grab your favorite high tech communication device and text or twitter #Jesus and as your inquiry is sent out across the internet, wait patiently while reading this book and see what happens!

Do not expect God to magically appear in an app, or for text to begin scrolling rapidly with messages of authenticity, but do watch and listen for a clarity of mind and understanding in your heart that will allow you to see clearly just where God is in your personal life.

It is my hope that you will discover how the answer came to one person (me) and that whether or not you find God will be entirely your decision without any pressure from anyone, any group, any church, any government agency, or any email or website. I offer through the pages of this book a unique opportunity for you to explore, compare, and decide if there really is a God and where in the world that God reigns! Do not read any further if you are not interested in learning how success can be achieved, in learning how peace can be experienced in chaotic circumstances, or in learning how you can survive through any unexpected trauma that might suddenly occur. I have discovered when you learn where God is, everything makes sense and a personal confidence brings understanding and excitement.

Begin with an open mind, begin with the knowledge that you have the freedom to stop anytime, and begin knowing this book is one man's freedom to say "WOW... LOOK WHAT GOD HAS DONE!" as he has reached 71 years of age in full retirement enjoying the fruit of a life that includes five children and fifteen grandchildren. You will see how an ordinary young boy with only the necessities of life gained peace and satisfaction, and in the process found the answer to that pressing question: #**Jesus… Are You There?** You will then discover how in one man's life, trusting God works!

#**Jesus,** hopefully, will become a reference for encouragement, inspiration, challenge, satisfaction, leadership, and motivation in meeting life's daily routine.

It begins with your author admitting he does not have all the answers or all the questions needed to achieve success in life. He has, however, reached a point in his life where he recognizes it is what he has done with the resources provided him that has caused him to mature into an age of satisfaction compared to a stressful push for everyday financial gain.

CHAPTER 2
#Jesus...
What Is It All About?

#Jesus...Wow... Trusting God Works is a story of a little boy, born into an average family of three brothers with hard working parents in a small Midwestern town, Greensburg, Indiana, known for its famous Tree on the Courthouse Tower. He lived the first twelve years of his life never knowing they were poor until a school buddy told him about a toothbrush in music class in Junior High School.

It is a story about little Bobby becoming Bob and then Robert over a course of life that stretches beyond his seventy-first birthday. He lives in retirement with a loving soul-mate, five children and fifteen grandchildren near the deep southern former Confederate Capital of Montgomery in Pike Road, Alabama, in an east-side suburban town.

It is a story of how one Midwestern lad lived through the aftermath of a society fueled with revenge to overcome the invasion of Pearl Harbor, watched two brothers proudly serve in the U.S. Army during the Korean conflict, followed his closest sibling through his U.S. Air Force commitment while preserving peace in Iceland, and then joined with the sailors of the U.S. Navy in the intelligence field proudly serving under Commander-In-Chief, President John F. Kennedy, during the tension-filled Cuban Missile Crisis.

It is a story of a boy, advancing to manhood as a father at twenty-one, starting work for $50 gross pay a week, asking for his first raise by showing a hole in his shoe, and moving frequently due to employment for gradually needed increases in pay to provide for a growing family.

It is a story of a young father who "felt the hands of God" upon his back during a small country church revival meeting about sixty miles from his hometown and who launched out in his quest to "do what God wanted him to do." Never entering the professional pastoral ministry, your author discovered how God can bless and use a man in any chosen profession.

It is a story of a middle-aged man dancing around a hospital bed with his wife of 33 years attached to chemotherapy IVs while singing "God Will Make A Way" only to discover that death would come just eight months and two days after the cancer diagnosis.

It is a story of a frightened man, trusting God for the future and learning that "God Will Make A Way" when he healed a broken heart with a new love that mended a broken marriage of a mother of two children seeking God's will in their lives.

It is a story of a man walking in obedience with God and in the process being blessed: adopting two sons, increasing to five children and now a family including fifteen grandchildren who live within a few miles of each other's homes.

It is a story of a man whose happiness is not measured by wealth of finances, but whose life is magnified by the blessings of a God who promised to "Make A Way," to provide all his needs (Philippians 4:19), and to never leave or forsake him (Hebrews 13:5).

It is a story of a man whose success is measured in lives strengthened through sharing of his life's spiritual riches.

It is a story of how anyone can live life to the fullest and endure it's trials and struggles when they put their trust in God.

Chapter 3
#Jesus...
He Never Changes!

The Bible teaches that Jesus is the same yesterday, and today, and forever (Hebrews 13:8), and that promise has been proven over and over through trusting the same God who provided my adversity, and the same God who delivered me from that adversity!

The same God who provided me life, provided me a loving family and friends, and provided me with food, shelter, and clothes. That same God who provided me salvation to live eternally is the same God who continues to make a way for me today.

God's unconditional love is the same for me in retirement as it was for me during a successful working career. It is the same for me in sharing love with my personal family and the same for me in sharing love with my homeless and street-living friends who have become my "barrel" family.

God provides the same loving direction of my paths from a growing little boy, an active teenager and young adult to the aging senior citizen still clinging to God's Word.

God continues to be a lamp unto my feet (Psalm 119:105) showing the way home in a society filled with darkness and shame, and He provides the reassuring love of compassion that counteracts the confusion of the world.

God still promises the abundant life to the obedient (John 10:10), and has paved the streets of Heaven in gold (Revelation 21:21) awaiting my entrance one day into eternity.

#Jesus ...Wow... Trusting God Works will implant within the hearts of the readers just what God meant when He promised to be the same yesterday, today, and tomorrow, and how His commitment can lead us daily through whatever life brings into our paths.

You will see just what God was saying when you lean not unto your own understanding, but in all your ways acknowledge Him and He will direct your paths (Proverbs 3:5-6).

The same God who took me two times to the cancer bedside of the ladies I loved most, not only provided me with the strength to go through that, but delivered me to the barrel of the homeless and gives me strength to love and obey.

God continues to provide a peace that passes all understanding (Philippians 4:7) in my heart while showering me with blessings of hope and joy as though each day is the most important to Him!

You are encouraged to compare your life and your success at meeting daily challenges that have either provided you with happiness or still has you searching for satisfaction.

Compare your dreams with your achievements, compare your hopes with your needs, compare your purpose in life with your goals, and compare your desire for success with your drive for peace.

You are reading a story with no answers or promises for success, but a story of how one man lived a satisfactory life.

How does the author know trusting God has provided satisfaction?

He has 71 years, plus children and grandchildren to

show; he lives each day with flexibility of time to do the things he deems important; he shares life with a loving wife; and he has pictures, pieces of priceless memorabilia, and countless stories of contentment in his life.

How does the author measure satisfaction?

Not with money, not with fame and fortune, but with a lifestyle that produces unconditional love and joy in the process of living each day.

Where did the author obtain the leadership and guidance to live such an exciting life?

He was reared by blue-collar, God-fearing and God-loving parents, given chores and household rules, taught family values and standards, raised as the baby of four brothers, educated in public schools, proudly served in the military intelligence field of the U.S. Navy, and lived a disciplined life of working in what he describes as the "most fun jobs in the world" as a newspaper reporter and photographer, a policeman, a radio news broadcaster, a play-by-play sportscaster, a manufacturing industry laborer, and as a banker prior to retirement.

What is so special about the author's life?

Nothing, except he flashes a big smile when asked to discuss his life. Nothing, except he cannot remember not having enough money for the necessities of life. Nothing, except he always tells how experiences and relationships along life's journey have prepared him for the next successful phase of life. Nothing, except he talks of the importance of learning in life to be "dependent" instead of "independent." Nothing, except his past reflects a history that has accumulated more than its fair share of blessings!

You decide!

It began with a smack on the bare behind from an Indiana country doctor on November 1, 1942, and it continues today with affirmation that this is a day that my heavenly Father has made and I am to rejoice and be glad in it (Psalm 118:34; Philippians 4:4).

Bob Bostic lives today guided by values and principles that motivate positive living.

How many men advance to senior citizen status and live within a few miles of all five children and fifteen grandchildren providing daily family blessings and challenges? It is especially noteworthy when you realize the family was reared in Midwestern Indiana, scattered for education and employment only to be reunited in one of the most unique southern state capitals, Montgomery, Alabama.

Job opportunities that located all the children in Montgomery was the draw that upon retirement brought the entire family to the deep South creating the unique and exciting lifestyle of sharing each other's activities and supporting each other's families.

Family history, traditions, and values emerge as huge blessings as a result of unconditional love networks that have strengthened what some have described as neighborhood family living.

Reading *#Jesus ...Wow... Trusting God Works* is dangerous! The author cannot be responsible for anyone experiencing a change in heart, a change in attitude, a change in their view of family values, and cautions everyone that a desire to enjoy life to the fullest might become a priority! Nor can the author be held accountable for any additional happiness that might come the reader's way from making positive changes in their lives.

Read on with anticipation, read with expectation, and read with excitement looking back to where you have experienced some of the same life events. Be prepared to discover a peace that passes all understanding as you continue your journey in life. It is my prayer that that biblical passage in Philippians 4:7 will come alive in your heart too.

Watch out, though! A burning desire to seek true happiness might come over you as the pages reveal one man's adventure in trusting God in all things!

Look for the things that proved to the author that God is real and that following in obedience to His Word has been a lamp illuminating his pathway as described in Psalm 119:105! Look for the times when the author could not possibly know what was ahead for him while experiencing disappointment, heartache, and success.

Find your own personal secret for living a successful life as you learn how the author met each day's opportunities. Make yourself a promise to: look for comparisons, look for similarities, look for end results, and look for direction in shaping your own life story.

May God open your eyes to His message for your personal life via the heart of a happy, satisfied guy named Bob Bostic.

#Jesus… Wow… Trusting God Works!

CHAPTER 4
#Jesus... Where Is God?

Where is God when ...?

That is a question that now motivates my faith, especially when I look back over my 71 years and realize God woke me up again today! But, how can I trust God if I can't see Him?

Some want to argue that God does not exist; but I have discovered in my life's experiences that God is real and very much engaged in my daily living.

So I think a good discussion for those who question God's existence is frankly to challenge those who believe in God to answer the question, "Where is God?"

As one who acknowledges God's presence in the world as Creator, King of kings, and Lord of lords, one who has accepted Jesus as my personal Savior, and one who has been blessed beyond measure by the grace of God, I am excited to accept the unbeliever's challenge!

Most would start by looking back over their lives, and although I have 71 years to scan for reasons, it is my strategy to look forward to something everyone knows and to start the discussion agreeing with each other. Looking ahead, one thing that cannot be argued is, "we all will one day die" and be left for final burial by our families, ending our life on this earth!

Ask yourself: If God exists, where is He? Where is He when we hurt, are disappointed, lose a job, see our families devastated by financial burdens, see children suffer through family divorce, a house burn down, a hurricane or tornado destroy our homes, tragedy kills a loved one, friend or neighbor, suicide takes a friend, thieves steal our belongings, poor health denies quality living, or loneliness pushes someone into becoming homeless?

Where is God when things are great, success is everywhere, happiness is obvious, money is plentiful, friends are endless, the food pantry is overstocked, everything we want is obtained, and our wish list keeps growing?

God is in each area of my life, both good and bad,

pointing to a discovery that the answer to the challenging question—Where is God when...?—is not so much aimed at finding the existence of a God we cannot physically see, but a realization that the presence of God is everywhere! We need simply to trust in Him.

I suggested looking ahead in agreement together to the day I die, remembering you will die too! I am excited that my life includes a belief and faith that on that day when life ends for me, my life will enter into a time of eternity that's promised in John 3:16 where the Bible says, "For God so loved the world, that he gave his only begotten Son, that whosoever believeth in him should not perish, but have everlasting life."

That day, the point of death, will also be a moment when you step into eternity. (I hope someday you will send me your thoughts on where you think you will spend eternal life after death. Save my email, **robert.bostic@yahoo.com**, and share your belief with me in the near future.)

I know where God is, where He has been, and where He will be in my life after death. You can decide where God is in your life as you read my opinion of "where is God?" in the different phases of my life.

Looking ahead is what convinces me God is real. I have experienced enough "ups and downs" that have served as evidence that He has been present in each good time and bad time.

How did my father, with a fifth grade education, whose home life forced him to be taken to foster homes at age nine when his mother could no longer provide for her five children following the death of her husband in the mid-1930s, support a wife and four boys on a janitor's wage? If you look close, you will notice that God was there around their table at meals, in that young boy's life as he promised his mother he would be back one day to get her as he walked down that country lane leaving for nine years of foster-home living. He was there when his dad went to live near a sister in Detroit so he could do industry work, and he was there when a farm hand job opened back home in Indiana where he settled and reared his family of wife, Thelma, and their four boys: Lester (Chick), Theron (Jim), Leland (Tom), and me.

How do I know God was there? The money wasn't, the "fancy extras" weren't, and fun vacations never existed, but I never once experienced a loss in family joy. Instead, I learned a work ethic that employers today would love to see in their applicants. I found it normal to eat from our garden. I couldn't wait to wear the shirt that my older brothers had worn. I cherished my one special gift at Christmas. I learned discipline from parents who gave me family guidelines and demanded obedience or suffer spanking consequences. I learned saying "grace" before eating was expressing our thankfulness for food being provided. I learned respect of parents who did whatever was necessary to feed, clothe, and give me a house and bed that became "home." Yes, God was there!

How do I know God was there when a little boy (me) survived three older brothers, waited patiently to "get his chance," grew to adulthood excited to excel, and start a family? I learned from the oldest sibling (ten years older) the value of getting a job at the mill to help purchase groceries and obtain that first car. I learned the tolerance of seven living in a four-room house with a kitchen and one bath and the difficulty of sleeping three boys to a bed with my oldest brother forced to share a bed with an uncle who was single and unable to care for himself. I learned sharing was normal, working together was necessary, and making the most of your time in the spotlight required an urgency to be prepared. Yes, God was there!

He provided me tolerance, comfort, protection, and care through the daily requirements of being the youngest in the family. Born in 1942 and being a teenager in the 50s, personal struggles for achievement were strengthened and family values were learned in the home. God was in the center of it all!

How do I know God was there when a friend at school whom I shared a desk with told me my breath smelled really bad and said he was sorry I was poor? I learned all work was important, even the janitor position my dad had at the elementary school and the job of cook that my mother held throughout my high school years. I learned it was not how many things we had in our home from the money my parents were paid that was important, but rather the fun in playing together, reading together, doing chores together, crying together, laughing together, playing brotherly tricks on each other, and helping each other was satisfying and important. Watching my brothers achieve motivated me, and I discovered love when I watched each leave home for military service; I felt lonely and wanted to be in their presence.

I learned to stand up for family values when I saw bullies push one of my brothers around. I learned to help my brothers out of trouble when I saw my brother Tom once circled by six guys on a football field and I jumped in the middle to do battle. I experienced the pride of brotherhood when two of my brothers proudly enlisted in the U.S. Army and one in the U.S. Air Force. I found it rewarding to follow their footsteps of defending our country as I joined the U.S. Navy. Yes, God was there when Mom hung her sons' pictures on the living room wall in their military uniforms. I saw and heard her prayers of thankfulness and protection as though she was talking to a God sitting next to her on the couch.

Printing class in high school provided me a talent/experience that the U.S. Navy recognized and sent me to a naval station that needed print shop sailors. A high school business teacher encouraged me to learn typing skills and that talent got me assigned to administrative duties where my proficiency earned the respect of commanding officers who led me into intelligence work and launched my successful Navy service. Yes, God was there when I was honored to meet Navy jet pilots dropping off aerial film taken over Cuba and secretly handling the administrative processing while photo lab personnel printed wall size photographs of the S.A.M. missile sites of the Cuban Crisis for President John F. Kennedy to study upon awakening each morning in the White House. Yes, only God could place a boy from Greensburg, Indiana, in such an important role where President Kennedy was making security decisions with the Russian officials in the early 1960s. I was honored to be on the intelligence team whose work was instrumental in providing photographic aerial information to the president. God was there!

How do I know God was present upon starting my working career following my military service? I need only reflect upon how the reputation of my hard-working parents, how the references of my school counselors, and being honorably discharged from the U.S. Navy was openly accepted by the publisher and editor of the *Greensburg Daily News* allowing me to become a reporter/photographer. Yes, God was there because I received the job although I had no professional writing or journalism experience!

Mom and Dad had taught me by example to work any job as though I was working for the Lord as encouraged in Colossians 3:17: "And whatsoever ye do in word or deed, do all in the name of the Lord Jesus, giving thanks to God and the Father by him." In following their advice, I was blessed to earn United Press International (UPI) top sports story, top feature writing story, and top photograph for the State of Indiana in the same year, opening future doors of employment that led me through newspaper, radio, industry, law enforcement, and banking careers that could have only been orchestrated by God.

How do I know God was in my career path? One

need only to know I had turned down my opportunity to attend college when I chose to follow the patriotic example of my hero brothers. The U.S. Navy rewarded my dedicated work ethic with exciting and important duty assignments and their educational opportunities prepared me for advancement and pay increases, disclosing and motivating my heart to the advantage and importance of life-long education. Yes, God was there as my career led me to earning Certificates of Law Enforcement at Indiana University; to Bank Marketing Certificates at Colorado University, and Bank Strategic Marketing at the University of Georgia; to an Economic Development Certificate at Ball State University, and a U.S. Chamber of Commerce seven-year Organizational Management Certificate at Notre Dame. Yes, it was God who took an ordinary boy and provided such a wonderful and satisfying educational lifestyle.

How do I know God has been with my family? One can know by looking into the faces of our five children, their wives, and our fifteen grandchildren at each meal or special occasions we share together; or perhaps by seeing college degrees on the wall of each child's home or office. Maybe we see it as our first grandson earned his college degree and is already within one year of finishing law school, our second grandson is completing his sophomore year of college, and our third grandson already is serving his country as an early recruit with the Alabama Air National Guard while a senior in high school.

Our fourth grandchild is already achieving professional theatre performances with a leading role in the famed Nutcracker Ballet while a senior in high school. Grandkids five, eight, and nine have earned stage championships in dancing. Grandchild nine is also a state gymnastics winner. Grandchild six just achieved all A's as a freshman in high school. Grandchildren ten and twelve are in first year swimming. Grandchild eleven is a first year gymnast who has already participated in helping to raise money for cancer victims. Grandchild thirteen is a miracle birth child born prematurely into neonatal care and is now living healthy and well, and grandchildren fourteen and fifteen are budding infants. Yes, God is definitely present and blessing in the growth of the Bostic family.

So where is God? I find Him each time I exercise my belief in Hebrews 11:1 from the Bible: "Now faith is the substance of things hoped for, the evidence of things unseen." I see God each time I look into the face of my wife, our children, and our grandchildren. I see God through each situation or circumstance of life, good or bad. I have learned that following the biblical teaching of Colossians 3:1-2 is key by discovering that although I can't see through my circumstances, I always find somehow that I was protected, comforted, and guided beyond those same trials and tribulations. Yes, "If ye be risen with Christ, seek those things which are above, where Christ sitteth on the right hand of God. Set your affection on things above, not on things on the earth."

I believe God answers my prayers, provides my strength for meeting the challenges of life, protects my family, honors obedience to His Word, and rewards eternally with grace and mercy. Though I cannot see, I know His loving Spirit is in my heart. I see His love each day in the rising sun's light and with the setting sun each evening, or the reflection of a full moon. Each new day brings another opportunity to find God in all things. This is a day the Lord has made!

It is my prayer that you yield your life to Jesus, walk each day knowing that all you do is blessed beyond measure by an Almighty God who lives unseen but present within your hearts.

Have you ever felt a comfort and a peace that you can't explain? Have you ever been afraid, but you overcame it when all seemed impossible? Have you ever achieved as though you were the strongest when you felt like the weakest? Have you ever failed but were uplifted by an understanding heart? Have you ever been tired but still succeeded?

What we cannot see is often revealed when it is all over. You are encouraged to "ask, and it shall be given you; seek and ye shall find; knock, and it shall be opened unto you" (Matthew 7:7).

May your future be blessed by the One everybody seeks to find, but cannot see! God is real, worthy of all praise, and very much alive!

Chapter 5

#Jesus ...
Is It Worth the Effort?

Have you ever wondered if trusting God is worth the effort?

Admittedly, I have! However, looking back, I can now see where God has transformed my frustrations into stepping stones that have led to receiving a life of satisfaction and peace. I use the term "receiving" because I have learned that I have "achieved" nothing without the grace of God Almighty "giving" it all to me.

I am motivated to write about the benefits of trusting God because I have been blessed to live long enough to see how He works in mysterious ways providing joy in my life that has proven to me His love for my attempting to obediently follow Him.

I remember how I wrestled with "trusting" or "doing it my way" and discovered the times when I followed

God's lead it yielded positive results compared to the negative results it yielded when I did it myself. Yes, there were times when I thought doing it my way was good enough, but only because I was lying to myself about the result I could have experienced if I had chosen God's path.

I hear this question from my Christian friends and I see it written on the faces of those trying to make right choices: Should I follow Jesus? Or should I keep this situation to my own choosing? This question comes when I reach a crossroads in life, when I am faced with a decision that will require me to give up something, or at a time when a personal commitment is needed.

Trusting is more than its definition of being inclined to believe or confide readily in something. It is giving up control of my own mind, and that is very uncomfortable. Trusting God is me allowing God to take control of my mind then acting upon His lead to meet the challenge at hand! The Bible teaches us to have the mindset of Jesus in Philippians 2:5: "Let this mind be in you, which was also in Christ Jesus."

I found most of my friends also struggle with that problem and felt God tugging my experienced heart to share how He has provided satisfaction and peace in my life in hopes that my story might encourage someone to follow Jesus and reap the benefits of trusting in God. Blessings have been showered upon me, an ordinary man who lived an ordinary life serving a real extraordinary, awesome God.

My story happily shares benefits of trusting God and the rewards it has given me as a little boy from Scoby Street in Greensburg, Indiana, educated in public schools, married to my hometown sweetheart, shown the world while in the U.S. Navy, and given fun and exciting jobs.

My life has not been perfect, nor has it been without bumps in the road. I encourage you to understand that satisfaction and peace are not results from never experiencing difficulties or troublesome times. They come from realizing God was alongside you, encouraging, pulling, pushing, praying, and hoping right decisions would be made when I became overwhelmed or was totally frightened in my daily life.

God has been and will always be as close to us as we want Him to be, even when we are totally unaware of his presence. I have learned God loves me and truly wants me to have the abundant life as described in John 10:10: "I am come that they might have life, and that they might have it more abundantly."

I know trusting God works because God is real!

Chapter 6
#Jesus... God Is Real

Don't be fooled! God is real ... but life is tough!

If trusting God works, why do we experience pain and suffering? How do we accept the pain of tragedy? How do we respond when news networks constantly deliver stories of unbelievable acts of violence and killings? How do we move forward in a world that sees political leaders and candidates turning our own citizens against each other for personal gain? How do we make life better when our hidden agendas prompt us to pass legislation calling for mandates that cannot be funded but require immediate implementation? How do we face a life that is filled with tough demands forcing life-changing decisions?

Where is God in all of this? Though He is very real and proven beyond a shadow of a doubt in Genesis chapter 1 and John chapter 1 of the Holy Bible to be the Creator of this vast world, how can one put trust in a love that permits such chaos and confusion?

Yet we live, we achieve, and we make it just like Philippians 4:13 says: "I can do all things through Christ which strengthens me."

Grandson Ethan (#10) was sitting next to me in church as an eight-year-old and asked, "How can you hear a God that you cannot see … and how does He speak to you, Granddad?" My reply was that Christ lives in your heart and when you decide to follow Jesus, He speaks to us through the Holy Spirit. It was an answer I pray Ethan will one day experience and explain to his children. I could see his eyes sparkling as he was analyzing all the pastor was speaking.

Answers seem to come from those who are painfully afflicted, from those in the middle of financial crisis, from those looking back, and from those at the end of a long, tough tunnel of affliction who are simply amazed they are still standing! Personal experience and a willingness to share stories of completion seem to be great teaching tools that will produce positive results.

I have learned God never said "accept me" and I will promise a life of fulfillment and happiness. I am reminded God said through His Son, Jesus, "Come, follow Me" as found in Matthew 4:19: "And He said unto them, Follow me, and I will make you fishers of men" as He began teaching a life of sacrificial love in serving others. Jesus, the proclaimed Son of God Himself was misunderstood, mistreated, rejected, beaten, and put to death in the cruelest form on a cross.

I have learned only cleverly written sales-oriented advertisements and commercials promise instant pleasure and success. Success and satisfaction requires long term commitments to action in applying principles for daily living compared to looking for what someone else can do for us.

It was President John F. Kennedy in 1961, who urged all during his inauguration address that Americans should "ask not what your country can do for you, ask what you can do for your country" as he attempted to inspire others to take control of their future by using their own personal strengths to achieve satisfaction. President Kennedy seemed to have an insight to success, but he himself was unfairly assassinated while serving as the 35th president of the United States.

God is not to be blamed when we fall short of expressing love and help to each other, and seem to move only when heartache, tragedy, financial loss, destruction, and death stops our lives in their tracks.

Don't be fooled, don't be discouraged, and don't stop

when you learn today is going to require a little more determination, more drive, more strength, and more time due to an unexpected event. Instead, find strength in knowing others stand ready to help you walk through any valley life provides us. Let me encourage you to read Psalm 23. It has been a source of strength to me many days.

Discover that God's words, "Come, follow Me," were a call to change our lives and to walk forward seeking every opportunity to help others accept anything life puts in their path.

Yes, don't be fooled; but do discover that *God is Real*, and He provides a way for us to live in a world destined to be tough with a promise of eternal peace.

Read with an open mind and heart the following testimonies of teenagers who were challenged by their youth leaders (my wife and me) to share how they came to realize God is real! Their short stories were first printed in a testimonial book, **GOD IS REAL**, written by the Senior High BYF of First Baptist Church in Greensburg, Indiana, that explores how trusting God worked for them. They represent only a few of the eighteen teenagers writing their personal testimonies for the publication.

Compare your life experiences and look at how these

teenagers talk of personal situations that continue to trouble teens today.

#Jesus... 1978

In this section, you will meet Rijn, Sally, Ron, Tim, Amy, Susan, Barb, Jim, and Don, members of that First Baptist youth group.

Rijn wrote: *I was on my way to Hell until Jesus entered my life. Instead, I am on my way to eternal life. I didn't get it (salvation) by anything I did. Not going to church, not helping people or anything else. Don't take my word for it, try God's [way]. Ephesians 2:8-9: "For by grace ye are saved through faith; and that not of yourselves, it is the gift of God; not of works, least any man should boast."*

Sally wrote: *When I was 10 years old, my mother became very sick. When I was 14, my grandpa died. I was really close to my grandpa so that's all it took to convince me that there wasn't a God. Grandpa was such a good Christian I couldn't understand why God let him die so I just told myself there wasn't a God. I went to Lake Forest as a teenager where I was told by my camp counselor that Christ was her best friend and He wanted to be my best friend too. I wasn't ready yet because I was still blaming God for letting grandpa die. One morning I opened my Bible and read 1 Peter 2:11: "Dear brothers, you are only visitors here since your real home is in heaven." I thought* about grandpa. Then I realized how selfish I had been. Grandpa was in Heaven with God where he wouldn't have to suffer anymore. I prayed to God and asked for His forgiveness.

On our last night, we sat down by the lake where a big fire was burning. I thought how God is like a fire. I need a fire to keep me warm. If I stay close, I'll stay warm. If I wander away, I'll get cold. I read Ephesians 2:13-14 in the Living Bible: "But now you belong to Christ Jesus and though you once were far away from God, now you have been brought very near to him because of what Jesus Christ has done for you with his blood; for Christ himself is our way of peace." God is like a fire. I was once cold and lonely, but now I've found the warmth of God's love and know the peace of having Him as my friend and Savior. I felt so happy and I knew there was a God. I thought, what is God to me? God is the promise of life forever. For though I may die tomorrow, I am only visiting this planet because my real home is in Heaven.

Ron wrote: When I was baptized and made Christ my Savior, that meant that no matter what happened to me, I would be assured of a place in Heaven. My Christian life was like walking with Christ beside me and close to me in the time of need. But He wasn't where He could do the most good, inside myself and in full control of my life. Christ is supposed to mean more than a person who saves us. He should become a personal friend, our master, and to *a certain extent, a way of life. I went to church on Sundays and lived in the world the rest of the week. Outwardly, I was a Christian, but inside I was essentially the same person I was before I was "saved": outwardly good but inwardly wicked like the Pharisee in Matthew 23. For seven years, I remained a spiritual body, not digging into the Word and establishing any sort of meaningful relationship with Christ. I decided to make Jesus Christ LORD and SAVIOR giving Him every aspect of my life to control. I became a new person following Colossians 3:5-11 — a new creation in Christ. I have since made many friends and, nothing short of a miracle, I have regained full hearing. There are going to be many bumps ahead, but I find assurance in knowing "I can do all things through Christ, who strengthens me" (Philippians 4:13).*

Tim wrote: *I guess I took God for granted most of my life. God was kind of a faucet to me. You turn Him on when you need Him and as soon as He meets your needs you turn Him off until you need Him the next time. God and I have had a lot of ups and down and I know that I haven't been a perfect Christian, but thanks to Jesus Christ He will forgive me for my sins and even forget I committed them. God means so much to me and especially when I feel down I can talk things over with Him and He always comes through. God does little miracles for me every day and I know without Him I am nothing.*

Amy wrote: *My parents took me to church, but it didn't* mean that much to me. I had been running with the wrong crowd and had been doing the wrong things many kids without Christ do and I didn't even realize it until I accepted Christ into my life. Then I looked around and saw my friends doing the same old things I used to do and I thought of how bad it really looked and how I really wasn't fooling anyone but myself. I didn't know which I liked to do the best: lie to my Christian friends or go on doing and acting like some of my other friends. At Lake Forest with our BYF group I realized that I didn't really know Christ as my personal Savior and that I had been lying to my friends and even to myself. James 1:22 says in the Living Bible, "And remember, it is a message to obey, not just listen to, so don't fool yourselves." I found out what it was to really live for Christ and not have to worry about anything. All we have to do is pray about our problems and trust God to take care of them. Colossians 2:6 says, "And now just as you trusted Christ to save you, trust Him for each day's problems; live in vital union with Him." I know that Christ is in my heart and soon I will be with Him in Heaven. I'm still going to be tempted, but I know and believe that nothing can separate me from God's love. Now I know what love really is because love comes from God and God is love. An awareness of God depends upon our response to His presence. He is perceived through eyes of faith and followed through the heartbeat of love.

Susan wrote: *As a child I went to classes for becoming a* *member of our church, went forward and was baptized. I was young and I didn't really know what I was doing. I didn't live according to God all the time even though I was brought up in a Christian family. At camp, I learned how to read my Bible and to pray. Jesus died on the cross to forgive us [of] our sins and all we have to do is ask for forgiveness and God forgives you. I know He's forgiven me of my past sins. Life isn't all roses after you've accepted Christ as your personal Savior. I have ups and downs and sometimes it seems there are more downs. But that is my fault because I haven't asked the Lord to help me. I'm still learning that you can ask Him anything, confide in Him, or just talk to Him when you're lonely or at any other time.*

Barb wrote: *I was brought up in a Christian home. But as I grew, I began to realize others in the church had something I didn't [have]. I had always felt that there wasn't any rush in accepting Christ as my Savior, but after being around Christian friends at camp, I knew there wasn't time to waste. I felt Christ reaching out His hand to me asking me to follow Him and to accept Him as my Savior. I was baptized in early September. I knew I had nothing to fear because Christ would always be there to protect me and guide me in everything I would do. I take Christ with me everywhere I go and ask Him to help me in everything I do, no matter how great or small the task may be. I just pray Christ will give us the strength from day to day to withstand the trials and tribulations for Him* *in the days to come and that each person may continue to grow spiritually and come to know Christ as I have before it's too late!*

Jim wrote: *I wasn't really accepting Christ as my Savior because I wanted to go to Heaven, but because I was afraid of going to Hell. I didn't grow in Christ. I knew I had a ticket into the game, but I didn't know that there was a difference between the sideline seats and the top row. I came home from camp with the Holy Spirit in my heart to direct me to live a Christian life. Returning to Lake Forest, I discovered that even though I had Christ in my heart, I lacked communication with Him and this was hindering my spiritual growth. I learned to have fellowship with Christian friends and how to witness to someone by not just telling them about Jesus but by also being a good example of a Christian to others. I learned to read the Bible and allowed Christ to talk to me through His Word. I accepted the challenge like eating every day, not just one day a week, seeking nourishment. And I learned prayer is the way Christians talk to God. One of my favorite verses is Philippians 4:13: "I can do all things through Christ, who strengthen me."*

Don wrote: *I was born 17 years ago a sinner just like everybody else in the world. And by the way, I'm still a sinner except now I have God in my life and I know He will forgive me. I've been going to church ever since I can remember. My parents made me go and I am glad they* *did. I remember when I used to play checkers down in the basement of our church and to show you how God has worked, my friend who played checkers with me, is going to be a minister and I'm going wherever Christ takes me — missionary, ministry, garbage collector, or wherever will be fine, just as long as I can share God with others. I got things straight with God at summer camp and ever since it has been like walking in a beautiful field with flowers all over after a morning rain in the spring. It has not been an easy road to travel, it has had some chuckholes in it, but I have confidence that God will see me through. I'm thankful that Jesus died on the Cross to save my sins so I may be with Him in Heaven. I don't see why this world is all confused and messed up when all they have to do is turn their problems over to God — Jesus. He's got the answer – Praise God!* (Special note on the success of Don: His current resume, now 36 years later, is evidence of how God has blessed a young man who committed his life as told in his own words above. Don has coached 28 All Americans in track and field, has coached 66 conference champions, has had 92 NCAA national qualifiers, has been voted four times as the Coach of the Year, and is currently coaching in a major Division 1 university on the East Coast. Yes, God heard the prayers of young Don and obviously has been directing his path.)

Chapter 7
#Jesus...
Seek God, Find God

Trusting God can only come after you have "found" God. Like most people who call themselves Christians, I thought finding God was simply going to church, singing in the choir, praying, listening to the preacher deliver a sermon, smiling at all the people around me, and shaking hands with everyone within reach.

I never realized it required making personal decisions, keeping commitments, seeing visions, and enduring pain and suffering. It took 71 years for me to finally comprehend that finding God has nothing to do with my attendance at church, but instead, my attention to His presence in the form of the Holy Spirit within my heart. Yes, I first received the Holy Spirit at age twelve when I accepted Jesus as my Lord and Savior, but did not fully discover his useful purpose until my life moved into the 70s. It was then that I developed a hunger to understand how and why my life has been so blessed and fulfilled when the world around me seemed so unstable and unhappy.

It is not that my life was any better than anyone else's, but rather my life continued to yield everyday excitement, challenges, and purpose when many the same age or younger seem so angry and perplexed with their lifestyles. First Corinthians 15:10 seems to apply directly to my lifestyle: "But by the grace of God I am what I am; and his grace which was bestowed upon me was not in vain; but I labored more abundantly than they all; yet not I, but the grace of God was with me."

Early in 2013, my Tuesday prayer buddies challenged each other to read a book a month, and in that process I became inspired by David Platt's *Follow Me*. In his book, I was challenged to begin seeking after God and to change my lifestyle from simply doing right things for God and begin actually following the guidance of the Holy Spirit working through me in trusting obedience to a Christ-like lifestyle that yielded my desires to those directed by God.

Living a life that was rooted in the love of a mom and dad rearing four boys through the depression of war and food stamps, I found it later to be a blessing that God made me the youngest of the Bostic boys, allowing me to benefit from the "battles" of older brothers, and using their experiences to help shape my choices. Although they kept their little brother at arms length and gave him the smallest part of the chicken at Sunday dinner (the neck), they were quick to offer advice that helped me make better choices than they did along life's pathway. Yes, as mentioned before, it was their example of serving our country in the U.S. Army and U.S. Air Force that made perfect sense for me to join the U.S. Navy and do my part at protecting the freedoms of our great nation.

Having loving parents who took me to church every time the doors opened with their personal commitments as leaders made perfect sense to me years later when I found myself as part of my church leadership team.

Yes, finding God started early for me. I just did not finally "get it" until looking back over a life that can only be described as having been truly blessed and guided by divine intervention of the Holy Spirit.

This discovery did not come with fame and fortune, wealth or riches, possessions or gifts, but instead it came only after overcoming the pains and struggles of normal life and maturing into a granddad who, if life ended in the next breath, would find himself smiling in the presence of God Almighty!

Wow… what a life! Find God; do not wait seventy-one years!

Here is a suggestion: Seek God studying.

Deuteronomy 4:29: "But if from thence thou shall seek the Lord thy God, thou shalt find him, if thou seek him with all thy heart and with all thy soul."

Psalm 63:1: "O God, thou art my God; early will I seek thee; my soul thirsteth for thee, my flesh longeth for thee in a dry and thirsty land, where no water is."

Jeremiah 29:13: "And ye shall seek me, and find me, when ye shall search for me with all your heart."

CHAPTER 8
#Jesus ... Marriage Till Death Do Us Part

Trusting God is essential to marriage!

The Bible records in the creation story in Genesis 2:24 that God points to a man leaving his father and mother to be with his wife, and in Proverbs 18:22 it is recorded that "whoso findeth a wife findeth a good thing, and obtaineth favor of the Lord." For some unknown reason in my life, God delivered that very blessing for me, Bob Bostic, to find not one good woman, but two!

The story is confusing because God blessed me for 33.5 years with Joanie, my high school sweetheart, and a life of unconditional love in marriage that ended only when that horrible disease, cancer, claimed her life just days short of her 52nd birthday.

I cried in lonely desperation while walking in

darkness in the middle of many nights with the family pet, seeking God's direction on moving forward alone, and asking for love to be withdrawn from my mind and my heart as I was searching for how to continue to live now that my Joanie was gone forever.

My children, especially our son, Matthew, the youngest who was a sophomore in college, and the only unmarried child still living at home, witnessed my heartache. Matt said, "Dad, what are you going to do? Live or die?" God was using my son to shake me into reality that I must move on or die. He had amazing insight to encourage his father to live looking forward, but remembering the past for strength. His sisters, Kim and Deb, gave family support encouraging my life with deeply inspired memories of their mother.

It was at the graveside that my heart settled on that answer as the Spirit of God opened my heart to the realization that death is the intended end for everyone. Ecclesiastes 3:1-2 says, "To everything there is a season, and a time to every purpose under the heaven; A time to be born, and a time to die; a time to plant, and a time to pluck up that which is planted." Also in Hebrews 9:27 it records, "And as it is appointed unto men once to die..."

Those words, "till death do us part," which everyone recites so smoothly, so eloquently, and so reverently at the marriage altar, pressed hard within my heart and I suddenly understood that God was revealing to me that life is to be lived to its fullest with high expectations and enthusiasm, giving 100% of the mind and soul to pleasing God together. It also helped me to understand that the day will come when the body will return to the earth from which it came. He revealed to me that Joanie's cancer had eaten up her body so much that when it became more than she could suffer, He answered our prayers crying out for healing by lifting her spirit to Heaven with the ultimate healing we all seek. Revelation 21:4 came to mind: "And God shall wipe away all tears from their eyes; and there shall be no more death, neither sorrow, nor crying, neither shall there be any more pain; for the former things are passed away."

It was like God was saying to me: "Bob, I see Joanie. I hear your cries to ease her pain and I will grant her reward into an eternity with no more pain or suffering and usher her into paradise, the same paradise I offered to those two thieves hanging on the Cross the day my Son, Jesus, was crucified, the same paradise you and Joanie told so many high school teenagers to seek, the same paradise you and thousands of others sing praises about each Sunday in church. Bob, you must live now in honor of the love you were blessed with for 33.5 years of marriage and 52 years of life as I still have more for you to accomplish for me."

Those words lifted me from praying with hands outstretched on the grass of that grave-site to a life of seeing my children finish their young careers and in the process see God not remove love from my heart, but re-fill it in a way misunderstood by many of my closest friends. In obedience to God, I prayed with my whole heart for His guidance and strength, and struggled with returning to an empty house. Turning into the driveway and garage became a very hard thing to do because I was so reminded each time how brokenhearted I was and how trying to move on seemed impossible despite the advice of a young assistant pastor in my community who prayed for me and said, "Bob, God one day will make you whole again!"

I was suddenly motivated believing Joanie was a hero of faith and that God granted her His promise of receiving ultimate healing in Heaven. I was again led to the Bible in Hebrews chapter 11 where heroes of faith are described. Verse 12 came to mind when I thought how God rewarded Joanie as I read: "These all died in faith, not having received the promises, but having seen them afar off and were persuaded of them, and embraced them, and confessed that they were strangers and pilgrims on the earth." Yes, that was the life of Joanie: she lived believing "God is good" and shared that message with all around her, even when her choice was not to be able to overcome a non-curable cancer. She allowed medical physicians experimental opportunities to use a bone marrow transplant that was risky but if successful would give her longer quality life and would for sure develop new research for future cancer patients to perhaps win their battles.

I was uplifted through the Holy Spirit reminding me of God's Word in Hebrews 12:1-2: "Wherefore seeing we also are compassed about with so great a cloud of witnesses, let us lay aside every weight, and the sin which doth so easily beset us, and let us run with patience the race that is set before us. Looking unto Jesus the author and finisher of our faith; who for the joy that was set before him endured the cross, despising the shame, and is set down at the right hand of the throne of God." I continue to choose that verse as motivation to keep my own focus on "looking for things ahead instead of things weighing me down!"

God used my love for two grandsons to lead me forward in His mysterious ways. Helping to coach/instruct my grandson Jason's beginner baseball team took me to the youth ball diamonds where I saw on an adjacent ball field a determined 12-year-old little leaguer hit a huge towering home run that directed my attention to his life. The ball he slammed over the center-field fence landed in the out-field of the game where my grandson was playing. What I saw was a boy who had a brother whom many of us in church, including my own Joanie, would pray for as they were caught up in a divorce within their family for several years. His mother was the choir director in our church and choral teacher in the local junior high and high school and was loved by many whom she helped during their difficult times. The other brother, Jason, was four years older and elected to stop playing sports because he accepted the responsibilities of helping his mom with the household and contributed his talents to the restaurant business to help make spending money.

My inquiries into young Jared's baseball skills led to discovering a path that God seemed to be placing those two brothers in my life as children in whose lives I should take an interest in making a difference. It was at a baseball game that their mother, Melissa, who respected me as a former banker in the community and then executive director of the community chamber of commerce, asked me for advice about the sale of a home she was considering buying. That conversation, those two boys, and what I now know was the Holy Spirit in my heart leading me forth, led to an invitation to dinner where God began the process of making me whole again just as the young pastor had predicted. I believed in 1 John 2:27, which states, "But the anointing which ye have received of him abideth in you, and ye need not that any man teach you: but as the same anointing teacheth you of all things, and is truth, and is no lie, and even as it hath taught you, ye shall abide in him." I believe the Holy Spirit was working in my life!

Although I prayed for God to remove love from my heart if that was His will for me, He convinced me at the graveside that the greatest thing I could do was to honor the love He had provided Joanie and me together by continuing to offer love in the future. The Holy Spirit within my heart gave me strength to openly and with integrity boldly move forward honoring God in the same manner Joanie and I had always done by living whole-heartedly for Jesus and doing what God directed in our hearts.

Although some wanted to judge my forward movement as disrespectful to my Joanie, I knew in my heart that we shared a love that I could not live without, and that God was again pouring into my heart a sweet favor that only a heavenly angel could orchestrate. Not many knew of how that around a hospital bed with the love of your life hooked to life-saving machines, we would sway back and forth in each others arms to the Christian love song "God Will Make A Way," and she would seek my promise to continue on and I, today, know without a doubt those lyrics were words intended for me, and my angel was foretelling the future.

Why would God heal a broken heart by placing a new love deep within that would lead a father to adopt two young sons and attempt to become a husband to a lady loved and respected by so many in the community? That question can easily be answered by seeing the fruit of the blessing as the Bostic family now has five children and fifteen grandchildren all living within a few miles of each other around Montgomery, Alabama. All the children have graduated from college. Grandson Jason also has his college degree and is currently in his third year of law school. Grandson Joshua is entering his junior year in college, and Grandson Zachary just graduated from high school but has already performed in three professional plays on stage and is entering a college known for its outstanding musical theatre programs.

Three granddaughters, Alea, Olivea, and Emmy, have won state championships in dance. Grandson Jacob graduated from high school earning two state championships in cross country and state runner-up in basketball and is now serving in the military with the Air National Guard of Alabama. Grandsons Jackson and McKay are achieving through freshman and sophomore high school academics. Grandchildren Ethan and Emmelyne are avid elementary swimmers. Grandsons, Trey, who is a gymnastics athlete, has already started giving of himself in shooting basketball for cancer victims, and Levi, Colt, and Knox are budding infants.

The entire family is a blessing that I may have never experienced if I would have accepted the temptations of Satan to just give up on life and stop being productive for Jesus when my soul mate passed away.

Yes, God not only provided the ultimate healing to our family, but He delivered what John describes in the Bible in John 10:10 as the abundant life to a man who listened to the Holy Spirit when reminded that "I have more for you!"

Melissa is the love of my heart in our second marriage and my co-servant in Christ as we give our lives to growing the Kingdom of God together. What a joy to pray and sing alongside my Melissa as we praise God with our service to Him.

You see, God also knew that Melissa would come down with cancer. Eight months after our marriage, Melissa underwent surgery for Stage 2 Breast

Cancer. Then eight years after being in remission following all those chemotherapy and radiation treatments, losing her beautiful hair, and taking those special medications, she was re-diagnosed with breast cancer on the other side and underwent surgery and treatments a second time. God knew she should not be alone and provided a way for me to share the burden and to love and support her in a manner in which he prescribed with my whole heart. Praise God, Melissa continues in healthy remission today and is openly sharing how she handles her cancer battle with others battling cancer.

Has it worked? The answer is in our hearts and evidenced in our lives where God continues to provide peace and satisfaction to a couple who finds joy in serving Him. Blessings abound as the love of God is showered upon our household. I thank God for His biblical promise in Hebrews 13:5 "to never leave us or forsake us."

Without a doubt, the love for Joanie lived deep in a heart that God expanded to be large enough to be refilled with the love of Melissa. Joanie entered Heaven on April 27, 1995. I believe she walks today along the golden streets praising our God. She would not want to come back. I walk today alongside and arm in arm with Melissa, the woman God abundantly blessed me with at a time I thought was the end.

Trying to understand how or why God would do all that hopefully will strengthen anyone seeking release to not give up or to stop living, and inspire them to live wholeheartedly as unto the Lord.

Marriage is a wonderful union ordained by God. Mark 10:9 says, "What therefore God hath joined together, let not man put asunder." Hebrews 13:4 says, "Marriage is honorable in all."

Thank You, Jesus, for the great things You have done. Wow! God blessed me two times!

Chapter 9
#Jesus ... Extraordinary Things

Trust God to do extraordinary things!

The phrase "an ordinary person doing extraordinary things" has been humbly used so often by speakers, pastors, and leaders in urging and motivating others to become involved, to make a difference, and to reach higher than expected goals in their lives.

That phrase more than describes my life as a little boy born down on that farm in Indiana, reared in that small community of Greensburg, and educated and encouraged to stretch farther and higher than my little 5-foot, 7-inch frame would reach.

That phrase accounts for the satisfaction enjoyed in learning the benefits of trusting God to lead me to the abundant life promised in John 10:10.

That phrase catches up to my retirement life where I can look back and wonder how this little boy traveled from that paper route bicycle journey all over town that put change in my pocket; to team vehicles heading to sporting events providing my first "tossed salad" at a baseball team meal; to the bus, train, and airplane travels while in the U.S. Navy experiencing life with no boundaries; to an exciting working career providing a comfortable life raising a family of my own; to the depths of my spiritual heart where I was privileged to serve on mission fields in Chile with the Chileans and in the mountains with the indigenous Mapuche people in south central Chile; to missions to the Dominican Republic where I was honored to minister to my first leper colony; to the country and tea mountain region of northeastern India where I was given opportunity to share the "Good News" of Jesus Christ while witnessing what true faith in God offers our lives; to faith exhibited in third world countries teaching the depth of God's love to those who choose to "follow Him" knowing many suffer life-threatening persecution and expulsion from their homes and families; and now, to the satisfying days of enjoying full retirement surrounded by family and friends.

That phrase came alive in many ways throughout my working years. A paperboy makes small change but that gave me snacks and movie tickets my family couldn't afford. My Navy career in 1960 started on a salary of $130 a month and $99 of it was required for my off-base housing to support my wife in starting our marriage together. My first working career job back in Indiana paid $50 a week of which I took home after taxes $30 and somehow we lived with our first child in a rented home that saw God providing food, shelter, and housing in ways that were quite extraordinary. I changed jobs, increasing income and benefits many times in adolescence, as God directed my paths to where I needed to be until landing a career position that became our rooted base for family growth.

Looking back, it is easy to see where God took an ordinary person (me) and provided and protected and gifted me with many extraordinary blessings.

I remember as a high school freshman watching my friends at graduation honor day receiving a special trophy for their accomplishments in baseball; a seed was planted in me saying "I want one of those" ... and it happened! I know now it was God putting friends around me, whom I not only had fun with playing a sport we loved, but I was being taught to recognize what I wanted in life and to set a goal to "go for it!" "Go" became a spiritual command to me that comes directly from God's word in Matthew 10:5-15 where Jesus commanded his twelve disciples to "Go" giving instruction to tell others of His love without fearing possible rejection. That provided me with strength to face difficulties that might be encountered while striving to reach life's goals. "Go" became an open challenge in my life, inspired by the promises and proof of God as written in the Bible.

Being small in stature was not an obstacle but instead an advantage to run faster, hit for singles, doubles and triples, and steal bases with enthusiasm. I remember my final high school baseball game was perfect at 5 for 5 at the bat in front of my parents at old dirt diamond Shriver Field. It was my baseball hero, Jackie Robinson, who inspired me to run fast enough that my hat would fly off my head between 1st and 2nd base in stretching a hit down the line. My dad loved it when that happened and I can still hear his chuckle in my ears as he shouted cheers of joy watching his youngest son achieve in even the smallest way. That has got to be what our Heavenly Father does each time He peers down and sees one of His children living in servant-hood obedience helping someone else in life.

I remember as a young rookie reporter going with my editor to a United Press International (UPI) newspaper awards banquet and seeing my peers get trophies for their journalism accomplishment. That planted another seed in me saying again "I want one of those." And I got it writing a first-place news story about a horrible airplane accident that killed 88 passengers aboard an airliner trying to land at nearby Indianapolis, Indiana. I got another first place UPI award for writing a sports story about a young senior player whose father died the afternoon of his sectional championship basketball game when he decided to play in honor of his dad that same night because "that is what he would have wanted me to do"...and his team won! Then God blessed me a third time with the first place state award in photography for community newspapers judging a human interest photo where I illustrated a young boy celebrating his thirteenth birthday playing beneath a ladder with a beautiful black cat that had a long curly tail crouched on top waiting to pounce on his shoulders at any unlucky moment.

I remember now how God used this ordinary little boy by putting a school counselor in his path where she could teach principles, ethics, and values that guided him as a young man unable to afford college into a world of learning an occupation that would be instrumental in his life forever. She saw I made my best grades in "printing class" and recommended me to the local newspaper where this ordinary boy became a young man educated "on the job" by printers, pressmen, and line-o-type machine operators planting a seed that would become a lifetime foundation for success.

The blessings followed me into the U.S. Navy where only God's protective hand guided me into a duty assignment that utilized my printing skills and launched a burning desire to achieve what continues today. It was all that special "on the job training" that, following my Navy tour of service, got me hired by the same newspaper that had trained me in the basement pouring hot metal for those line-o-type machines. This time they hired me as a reporter-photographer! (Another example of just an ordinary guy getting an extraordinary job.) The future led to that night of three first-place top Indiana UPI awards where my proud newspaper owner/publisher was asked two questions: Is Bob your son? Did he get his journalism degree from the famed journalism school Indiana University? To their surprise, the answer was "no." Just an ordinary guy doing extraordinary things!

Life is a mission and what joy I have learning that trusting God would provide for me "extraordinary things!"

Chapter 10
#Jesus... Jobs

Trusting God has provided jobs that have not only shaped my life, but jobs that have delivered to me more than money. It has paid benefits that have allowed me to not just use the talents and skills to do the job, but to be prepared and positioned in life for whatever that season of my personal lifetime needed or required.

The Scripture teaches God will meet all our needs in Philippians 4:19, and looking back over my career, it can clearly be seen that putting trust in His word has provided at all times for the Bob Bostic family.

A friend as close as a brother, Hugh Chambers, always shares a smile and joy with me when it is evidenced that God provided "just enough" in another key moment in our lives as we raised our families in the same neighborhood together.

It was my first real career job that led to meeting

that special friend after my wife took a neighborly cup of tea over to the new neighbor housewife, Jewell. They had moved to the block just across the street. The wives met drinking tea together not knowing that their husbands had met at a fatal car accident along a two-lane highway about five miles from the city limits. Hugh, who turned out to be the best Christian friend a person could have, was an Indiana State Police Trooper investigating an auto wreck which claimed the life of a prominent retail business owner. We met as I was taking photographs of the accident as a rookie reporter/photographer for the local newspaper, *The Greensburg Daily News*.

It proved to be an assignment that God would bless and strengthen as two individuals shared common interests in serving the public as a state policeman and as a journalist. That camaraderie stretched into, not only sharing exciting and often times unbelievable stories of human interest, but loving and memorable discussions about the many blessings God bestowed on both our families in that hometown environment. That friendship created a bond that now includes over fifty years of interaction between our two families.

It is easy to see that God not only gave me a fun and action-packed career, but provided a friend who would become an accountability brother who would be used by God to keep reminding me of that precious promise in Philippians 4:19 by pointing to the many times when we always had "just enough" to make it through. Yes, Hugh and I have seen many times when "just enough" came unexpectedly at the right moment.

God started His shaping of my personal career mold when teachers picked me out of a 5th grade classroom and said, "Your dad has brought a visitor for you to meet." You see, my dad was janitor at the school and my mom was a cook at the same school. He had earned high respect from all my teachers, and if Mr. Bostic needed to see his son in the hallway, they knew without question, that it was for a good reason. I think Dad had convinced this particular teacher after the day that he called me out of class to be punished for being the unruly boy who laughingly kept knocking gravel out of a buddy's pant leg cuff while climbing up three flights of stars on the way back to class after recess. At least it seemed to me that not just the teacher, but the classroom students also enjoyed watching me forced to not only pick up all trash on the school yard, but also to sweep clean every stair step in that old castle-style school house.

However, this time dad had a surprise for me. A man dressed in a suit with the smell of cigar smoke all over him shook my hand and invited me to become a "stringer" reporter for the *Cincinnati Post*, covering high school basketball games. Keep in mind that he was not only looking for a "newspaper boy" to deliver 50 huge papers on all sides of the community, but along with it was a need for someone to go to all the high school basketball games and use a phone to call in the final scores and the "box score" statistics of the game so they could include Greensburg High School in their regional coverage on the sports pages of the *Cincinnati Post*. Yes, I accepted the newspaper route job, but what I truly accepted was the opportunity to keep score for the Greensburg Pirates, a joy that took me from 1951 at nine years of age until 2013 at seventy years of age when my heart was blessed with watching that same high school basketball team finally win a coveted Indiana state basketball championship. It was such a great moment God had provided and I considered it a treasured joy to drive on the interstate heading back home from Alabama (where I live in retirement) from 3 pm on a Friday non-stop until 5 pm on Sunday. Traveling with three grandsons and one grandson's beautiful fiancée and sleeping overnight with dear friends made it all enjoyable and possible!

I learned in that first paper route job the importance of working as though I was doing it unto the Lord and to give one hundred percent effort because many evenings my small boy body was not big enough to haul those big city papers in my bike basket without it always tipping over. The quicker I could pedal those sidewalks, the lighter I could make that basket and get home to more fun things. One lesson I learned was the best way to handle difficult situations, especially when you discover something scares you and puts your life in turmoil, was to face the issue and not cover it up.

For weeks I delivered newspapers as a loyal newspaper boy to a home on a lonely dead end street that was heavily shaded and led to a cemetery. The residents were wonderful, but every time I hopped off my bike to collect the weekly bill for the paper, there was this big dog taller than I jumping against the screened front porch door barking and salivating through its big white teeth and obviously not carrying any money for me. Week after week I personally paid that bill out of my carrier money because I thought delivering the paper was something I had agreed to do and therefore I shouldn't stop. My supervisor boss in that cigar-smelling suit thought it was good of me when learning of the situation, but quickly encouraged me to simply stop paying their bill for them.

That devotion to duty despite working under conditions less than favorable to me seemed worth it just to get the opportunity to be that "stringer" reporter on the weekends who launched a career that continued even in retirement.

That reporting interest that led to returning home from military service in the U.S. Navy to begin a working career in my hometown as a news and sports reporter-photographer and that took me out on that first assignment to cover/report on that fatal accident where that state trooper named Hugh became my Christian brother for life, was an affirmation of how God was in control even at age nine in the life of a little Midwestern boy.

Jobs within newspaper and radio led to a banking position that allowed continuation of sports journalism because of the close relationship to community bank marketing that permitted night-time sports broadcasting assignments. Also, becoming a police officer opened up opportunities to share community values that can still be seen in my retirement today.

Retiring from banking in 2005, God continued to provide "just enough"—not just in money for the bills, but in a fun, challenging, and exciting lifestyle that uses all the gifts and talents achieved along the way. Sports, yes, as this season was my fifth year to have the joy of being the public address system announcer for all the men's and women's basketball games for Auburn University Montgomery campus. Banking, yes, as I am in my second term serving on the MAX Credit Union Leasing Operations Committee. Journalism, yes, as I am in my fourth year of writing about ministry service to the homeless and street folks of Rosa Parks & Stone Street in Montgomery, AL. Radio, yes, as hometown WTRE-AM 1330 continues to allow me to share stories on the Pirates' basketball broadcast team every visit back to Indiana. Police, yes, as I have completed a four-year active term and am a past president of the Central Alabama Crimestoppers in Montgomery.

All have been surrounded by the greatest joy of life in serving within a Godly church that allows my job knowledge and skills to transfer into life applications within the teaching structure of the church. It all dates to being raised by God-loving parents, Delta and Thelma, taken to church every week, encouraged to work with my whole heart, and watching God unfold experiences that sustain life even today!

Wow! Trusting God works!

Chapter 11
#Jesus...
Today, Tomorrow & Forever

Is there a need to trust God everyday?

Living in Montgomery, AL, in the east side of the city, a person finds each day brings choices that will govern their individual happiness for that day. If you depend upon just yourself it proves to be very dangerous and risky in making the correct decisions.

Learning today to only please myself will not promise me a tomorrow of happiness or a successful future.

Learning today to please others will give me a promise of a tomorrow of satisfaction and a future of hope.

Learning today to use my abilities for the sake of someone else will give me a promise of fulfillment and a future of peace.

Learning today who to serve, promises me a challenge to press forward tomorrow and will give me a promise of accomplishments forever.

Learning today to never apologize for seeking God's direction in my life promises correct choices tomorrow and assures a life of joy in all things.

Yes, I have discovered trusting God today for tomorrow is essential!

To help understand, compare the same questions to your marriage or to your special relationships. If married, can you possibly have a great life together with your spouse if you choose only to love each other every "once in a while"? In your special relationships with family or friends, is it possible to remain strong in your devotion to each other "only once a week" or maybe "only a few times a year"?

To experience satisfaction and happiness, I have learned to follow and trust my Jesus everyday and in return receive the spiritual reward of having Him guiding me in all of my life's decisions.

Has it worked?

I am convinced the same God who created the world as described in Genesis 1 and John 1 is the same God who blessed me living in a household as the youngest of four boys.

The same God who found favor in Noah in Genesis 6, at a time when God was so grieved in His heart to declare in Genesis 6:7 that He would destroy man whom He had created from the earth, and who instructed Noah to build an ark to survive the 40-day flood in order to replenish the earth with a fresh beginning, I believe is the same God who blessed my mother with a fifth little boy after suffering a miscarriage of her fourth son two years prior to my birth.

The same God who led Abram at age 75 into the land of Canaan in Genesis 12, promising "to make of thee a great nation and make they name great," is the same God who gifted me with a son eight years separated from his two sisters at a time of life when "no more children" were planned.

It was God who delivered Joanie from her cancerous disease to perfect eternal life and it was God who healed two broken hearts and joined Melissa and her two sons to my blessed life.

The same God who strengthened David to kill the

giant, Goliath, in 1 Samuel 17, and who forgave David of his lustful sin in 2 Samuel 11, is the same God who David called "my rock and my fortress and my deliverer" in 2 Samuel 22:2, and is the same God protecting and guiding me as my Lord and Savior.

The same God who lifted the young dreamer, Joseph, from death's pit into King Pharaoh's palace where He was "blessed" to save his family from death due to severe drought and famine in Genesis 37 through Genesis 50, is the same God who provides daily food, clothing, and shelter to my homeless friends in west Montgomery, AL, and who has delivered a satisfied life of contentment to me despite personal and financial loss.

The same God who protected Moses from death as a baby, who rescued Moses a second time at the "burning bush" in Exodus 3, who called the ground Moses stood upon "holy ground" when directing him "to bring forth my people the children out of Egypt" in Genesis 3:11, is the same God who directed me to get up from mourning at the grave-site and go forth living a life blessing His name!

The same God, today, allows mankind to make choices that are personal and self-serving and continues to offer love and guidance to His faithful followers.

The same God who proclaimed man falls short of the glory of God in Romans 3:23 is the same God who today offers the opportunity "that if thou shalt confess with thy mouth the Lord Jesus, and shalt believe in thine heart that God hath raised him from the dead, thou shalt be saved," in Romans 10:9. He is the same God who freely gives eternal life in John 3:16, "For God so loved the world, that he gave his only begotten Son, that whosoever believeth in him should not perish, but have everlasting life."

He is the same God who today promises in Romans 10:13, "For whosoever shall call upon the name of the Lord shall be saved."

My encouragement comes from the Bible. Isaiah 12:2 says, "Behold, God is my salvation; I will trust, and not be afraid." Jeremiah 7:4 says, "Trust ye not in lying words." Jeremiah 9:4 says, "And trust ye not in any brother." Micah 7:5 says, "Trust ye not in a friend." Second Corinthians 1:9 says, "Should not trust in ourselves." Psalm 118:8 says, "It is better to trust in the Lord than to put confidence in man."

I know in my life, God is definitely the same today, tomorrow, and forever. The key for me has been simply "trusting"—yes, trusting Jesus to be the same today, tomorrow, and forever!

Chapter 12
#Jesus... Friends

Trusting God provides friends closer than a brother. Proverbs 18:24 declares "and there is a friend that sticketh closer than a brother."

Satisfaction comes as a result of outcomes of life's experiences and along the path it is discovered that "friends" play an important role in shaping those successes.

Friends may have been the shoulder you cried upon, hugged with excitement, wrapped your arms around in times of fear, and relaxed with at the end of an exhausting day.

Friends may have been the ones who gave the encouragement when everyone else was judging or pointing fingers, the one giving strength when your own had run out, the one finishing the job when your effort was unexpectedly halted, or the one interceding with doubters when at your lowest point. God gives assurance in Proverbs 27:17: "Iron sharpeneth iron; so a man sharpeneth the countenance of his friend."

Friends may have been listening with a compassionate ear when you unloaded a burden; they may have been available for immediate response when no one else seemed interested in your story; they may have been the understanding pillar when truthful details didn't shock an open heart; or they may have been the one to step even closer when being yourself was not being accepted. Ecclesiastes 4:9-10 says, "Two are better than one; because they have good reward for their labour. For if they fall, the one will lift up his fellow; but woe to him that is alone when he falleth; for he hath not another to help him."

Friends may have been the difference in moving forward instead of running, the difference in standing tall instead of hiding behind your past, the difference in speaking up instead of shutting down, and the difference in living and dying. Friends often reflect Christ-like characteristics of biblical values as described in Proverbs 17:17: "A friend loveth at all times."

Friends are another sign of personal riches and satisfaction! Trust God to be your best friend and discover life filled with spiritual strength and guidance. It is my suggestion you follow the advice of John 15:14 where it is recorded that Jesus said, "Ye are my friends, if ye do whatsoever I command you."

Trusting God you can find comfort, peace, and joy from a loving God who sent His only begotten Son to die on a cross to provide an abundant life to those who accept His love and follow His teachings (John 3:16 and John 10:10).

Yes, God is the ultimate friend! One need only to read John 15:13 where Jesus spoke not only truth but issued a challenge: "Greater love hath no man than this, that a man lay down his life for his friends." Jesus died for me, forgiving all my sins and I have learned I should seek and be the same friend "that sticketh closer than a brother."

Where do you find these special friends? Try your local church where small groups are offered in their teaching program and discover how "special bonds" will be made as you pray together, sing together, laugh together, study together, lift praises to God together, help others less fortunate through special projects together, and as you broaden your world of vision through planning together. I enjoy not only sitting in church worship with friends, but also singing in the choir, Bible study, a noon time men's prayer lunch, a breakfast men's prayer team and a Tuesday noon Bible study/worship lunch with special homeless friends.

Yes, friends are priceless! Trusting Jesus is priceless!

Personally, I love the old hymn my mom and dad used to sing when they "dragged" me to church with them: "What A Friend We Have In Jesus!" He certainly is mine! He has delivered many friends that I have seen grow even closer than a brother just like the Bible promises!

There was Roger, a friend I played with in elementary school so close we would take turns "staying overnight" with each other's families until one day his dad changed farm jobs and moved away. I missed our special friendship thereafter, but I know our doing so many things together developed in my young heart the importance of having a friend you could not just learn with at school but could also share dreams, play imaginary games, conquer what seemed unreachable desires, and find peace in simply being together experiencing the world of little boys.

There was Eddie, a special friend who was in a wheelchair and we would go outside for school recess and I discovered how happy he became when I would play pitch and catch with him, when I would see that he was included in our games, even pushing him to first base when he would attempt to hit the ball at bat on the school yard. Eddie became crippled because of his terrible muscle disease and I missed him when he could no longer come to school. I know now it was Eddie who without trying placed love in my heart for the less fortunate, something only a friend can do without even trying!

Wow! There was Doug, Max, Bob, Dick, Nolan, Steve, Louie, Paul, Bill, Maury, Charlie, David, John, and countless other friends on all sides of town who helped shape my life.

Not only did both of my parents work at the school as janitor and cook, but they were leaders in their church, and this provided many opportunities to interact with friends because everyone in our small town knew the Bostic family.

I learned, sometimes the hard way, the old saying "It takes a community to raise a successful boy" was a blessing when God provides working parents.

Friends taught me while climbing trees, playing sports, cutting grass, picking berries, joining the YMCA, going on overnight camp-outs, fishing, boxing on the summer playground, engaging in kids' club activities in backyards, and even raising funds for ball uniforms by selling popcorn door-to-door in the neighborhoods. I learned many important life lessons.

It was friends, Louie and Bill, who pledged to join the Navy together launching a tour of military service that helped us grow into responsible young adults. We each returned to our hometown starting our families together.

Yes, lessons learned from youthful and adult friends were truly the blessing that encouraged and pointed my life in the right direction for success. God knew my parents needed all the help they could get in raising little Bobby. It was even Mom and Dad's friends, Martha and Bill, who gave me my first swimming lesson in a big oversized farm horse tank!

I don't think I knew it while growing up, but God placed each friend in a season of my life providing the camaraderie, the comfort, the accountability, the compassion, the encouragement, the constructive criticism, the prompting, the prodding, the congratulations, the applause, the suggestions, and the rebukes that kept my life on course moving forward.

Melissa is my best friend now, and I know our life

together has been made better because so many dear friends chose to pray and ask God to heal and bless our broken hearts and our families.

Mom and Dad were absolutely correct! If you want to have a good friend you need to be a good friend, and following the example of Jesus is how it is done.

I am so glad Mom and Dad "took" me to that small church where everybody would sing aloud, "What A Friend We Have In Jesus." They would sing *what a privilege to carry, everything to God in prayer.* Friends provide the joy of always being there for you.

They also sang *"Jesus knows our very weakness."* Friends discover all there is to know about you often saying the right thing at the right time.

That church would also sing about being *weak and heavy laden, cumbered with a load of care.* Friends allow you to "unload" and get off your chest things that need to be released.

I can still hear voices loudly singing *do thy friends despise, forsake thee? Take it to the Lord in prayer.* Friends, despite their good and important qualities, are still humans who sometimes can disappoint and let us down and that old church hymn reminds us that God will always *take and shield thee.*

It just could be that when your friend is letting you down, you need to be a friend! That's what Mom and Dad told me.

Wow, they were so smart! Thanks, Mom and Dad, for teaching me "What A Friend We Have In Jesus" written by Joseph M. Scriven. I'm reminded of Exodus 33:11 when God spoke to Moses as a friend, and in John 15:13 where the Bible says, "Greater love hath no man than this, that a man lay down his life for his friends."

Following my parent's example, I now add another favorite church hymn: "No One Understands Like Jesus," lyrics by John W. Petersen. It has taught me *He's a friend beyond compare.* In my darkest times, *tenderly He whispers comfort, and the broken heart He heals.*

Jesus wants to be your friend that's closer than a brother. He gave His life for you and for me! He wants to be your Lord and Savior!

CHAPTER 13
#Jesus... Disappointments

How do you trust God through disappointments?

Along the way there have been plenty of disappointments but none so discouraging to stop life!

Despite living in a society that demands perfect living, it is tough to balance what affects one's life when compared to the life others want us to live! Parents want children to avoid the tragedies or pitfalls they themselves fell victim to, avoid the growing pains of competing for one's spot in life, avoid the lessons only saying "no" can provide, and attempt to make anything short of winning a failure.

Despite living in a society that encourages climbing to the top at any expense to your peers, gaining personal success regardless of who needs to be shoved out of the way or whose toes need to be stepped on, telling only half-truths when it comes to giving honest feedback to those in authority over us, and grabbing all the credit when accomplishment actually came at the work of a team effort.

Despite living in a society that rewards the aggressive, the line jumper, the influential recommendation, the blood line of a coveted family tree or the special interest money nudging out a more qualified person for the position, the longevity of life far outlasts the temporary time-frame of an always changing society and the short-lived seasonal success of personal gain at any cost.

Society sometimes leads one to make life-threatening decisions when one is coerced into comparing one's happiness and wealth with one's peers. I have learned that attempting "to keep up with the Joneses" has proven financially dangerous!

Disappointments become learning experiences for moving forward and reshaping lives one day at a time.

Trusting God, learning to accept disappointments, making positive adjustments with disappointments, and looking for the opportunity to increase knowledge in disappointments can lead to an attitude that disappointments can become yet another sign of coming satisfaction.

Trusting God overcomes the fear of disappointments, makes disappointments a challenge for adjustments in life, and provides peace of heart knowing God is in control. For me, trusting 2 Timothy 1:7 provides confidence to face each day: "For God hath not given us the spirit of fear; but of power, and of love, and of a sound mind."

Trusting God has brought to me a life that is measured by satisfaction rather than wealth. Don't get me wrong. I, too, enjoy what money can buy, but I have learned to beware that the Bible also teaches "the love of money is the root of all evil" as written in 1 Timothy 6:10. Chasing only money and fortune can force a person to make wrong life-wrenching decisions. Society, without personal discipline, can provide only disappointments that will prove devastating. Trusting God can provide real, life-sustaining satisfaction.

I choose to trust God's Word in the Book of Philippians. Chapter 4:11 says, "Not that I speak in respect of want; for I have learned, in whatsoever state I am, therewith to be content." And Chapter 4:19 teaches, "But my God shall supply all your needs, according to his riches in glory by Christ Jesus."

Yes, trusting God with my disappointments has

delivered peace of mind and a satisfied life!

I was disappointed when I was cut from the high school basketball team as a sophomore because I was too short. But, I learned a determination to succeed by playing YMCA basketball with diverse age teammates in developing personal skills that made me battle to overcome my height shortcomings.

I was disappointed to always be chosen for team sports only after all the bigger, stronger boys were selected, but it awakened my inner sense to play harder and run faster than others to earn my way. Once respected, disappointments became rare exceptions.

I was disappointed when Mom and Dad would not let me stay home alone, when they would expect my chores to be done before I went out to play, and when they would make me go to church when I did not want to go.

I was disappointed the day my dad made me miss a neighborhood baseball game because he made me pick strawberries on my hands and knees while my friends were playing. Dad knew the strawberries were "ready" for picking and baseball could be played another day. I recalled that story when as an adult I raised watermelons and the night I saw them ripe for picking I chose to wait one more day because I had something else I wanted to do for myself. I went to the watermelon patch down along a hillside by a creek that flowed through our property the next morning only to find someone had stolen all the watermelons knowing they were "ripe for picking" the day before! Dad was always right!

I was disappointed when my dad could only afford an old used car that was so ugly and unreliable. In fact, he owned two identical cars: one to supply parts to keep the other one running. That car was an embarrassment to me, and, one evening, when Dad was taking me to a high school youth meeting at church, I asked him to simply "drop me off" at the corner a block away so other kids could not see our car. Dad never said a word but he kept driving around that corner, veered over on the sidewalk, and pulled the car up next to the front door steps honking the horn and waving to all the kids who also heard him say, "Have a great time!" I learned to never be ashamed of what we had and grew to appreciate all the things that God provided our home.

I was disappointed that Mom and Dad never had very many "extras" in their lives, never could take our family on a fun vacation except to visit relatives in other towns, yet, they never seemed to complain.

I learned my disappointments came from loving Mom and Dad so much that I wished I could have made their lives easier. It also motivated me to excel in ways that seemed impossible remembering how God taught in the Bible, "all things are possible to him that believeth" (Mark 9:23).

My disappointments have taught the value of trusting a God who loved me so much He sent His only Son to the Cross for my sins, a God who made Delta and Thelma my parents, and a God who promises "but seek ye first the kingdom of God and his righteousness; and all these things shall be added unto you" in Matthew 6:33.

When I really think about it, disappointments have always stretched my thinking, showed me how to overcome, and kept me focused on how I could do better.

Trusting God works!

Chapter 14
#Jesus… Eternal Happiness

Download Jesus then upload your heart into eternal happiness!

#Jesus, or some other streaming path on the internet, might be the best way to communicate in the world of the 21st century, especially if you are looking for the answer to the question, "If you should die tonight, where would you spend eternity?"

We live with technology that is so quick that an answer can come at the touch of a finger or even the sound of a voice before you can finish the question. However, that one question about eternity still demands personal commitment, action, and trust in a manner it did over 2,000 years ago. Today, we have many ways to communicate, and the most direct is within one's own heart and mind.

#Jesus is non-threatening, easy to download, and you really do not need to purchase a special iPhone, iPad, tablet, droid, or sign up for a two-year contract to get a discount. It is voice-activated: all you need do is say the name JESUS and He begins answering. Lift your voice to Jesus and your connection is made even quicker than today's internet instruments utilizing the best of cyperspace. It will be faster than your shortest "tweet."

#**Jesus** has no cell outages, no boundaries or towers, and stretches around the world! You need no battery, no special cords and no need to download additional apps to receive the top program from the heavenly app store. You do not even need to choose a special package to get the most direct signal and everything is clearer than the most advanced HD offering. Access results in unlimited data and all applications are totally free as a gift from God. Some great news is that you don't need to text or search web pages. Connection requires only prayer activation.

#**Jesus** allows you immediate access to the Creator of the world, using a direct line of prayer expressing your inner thoughts without fear of someone hacking your password, stealing your identity, or depleting your financial accounts.

#**Jesus** releases the Holy Spirit within one's heart enabling powerful unlimited success.

#**Jesus** is calling. He sends a simple message of eternal love and never stops beaming His signal.

#**Jesus** is today's challenge to a nation searching for peace. The answer is simple but requires faith—believing the inspired writings of the Bible. Psalm 55:22 is a prime example of what happens when you upload your needs, desires, and burdens, and download a blessing described in Scripture as "Cast thy burden upon the Lord, and he shall sustain thee." Psalm 91:15 says, "He shall call upon me, and I will answer him." This encourages all to upload a prayer and download peace of mind, knowing God has promised in His inspired words in the Bible to answer.

I found strength knowing Isaiah 65:24 is further proof that God is waiting as it reads "And it shall come to pass, that before they call, I will answer; and while they are yet speaking, I will hear." I discovered God already knows my upload and is already downloading His will for me.

#**Jesus...Eternal Happiness** is as close as #**Jesus**. Receive the "Good News" of Jesus in John 3:16 by accepting God's free gift of love delivered when His Son died on the Cross, was raised from the grave, and provided our promise of eternal life in Heaven. Find peace in Philippians 3:20, where the Bible declares, "For our citizenship is in Heaven."

The answer to that age-old question, "If you should die tonight, where would you spend eternity?" is simply calling upon the name of Jesus, accepting by faith He died for the sins of the world, repenting and asking for forgiveness, and receiving the Holy Spirit in your heart with the assurance that "your citizenship is indeed in Heaven."

Unlike the most modern high tech internet device in society, no money is required to download through #**Jesus.** It is all free for the asking!

Wow … be happy!

CHAPTER 15
#Jesus... He Provides

When you trust God you learn that God will make a way ... no matter what!

Living in retirement since 2005 has not been living on "easy street," but the principles that I learned during my childhood back in the "good old days" continue to motivate and satisfy my life at a time when society is searching for ways to be successful and to find happiness.

Yes, being reared in that Midwestern town with blue collar parents earning just enough wages to make ends meet, learning values of a God-fearing family, and being educated in disciplined public schools, proved to be keys to developing a satisfied lifestyle.

That end result is claimed only after learning through life's journey that one will experience many "ups and downs," detours, distractions, disappointments, heartaches, and discouragements along the way; but in each case for me, God made a way, and that lifestyle provided fulfillment and satisfaction.

Being poor, small in stature, and the baby of the family provided a background of overcoming, standing up to challenges, and a motivation to excel which contributed to achieving a satisfied quality of life.

God made a way to overcome all the hurdles and challenges of youth. God made a way to educate a young man without funds. God made a way to provide for marriage and family. God made a way to work and earn family income. God made a way for overcoming the death caused by cancer of my wife, my high school sweetheart, after 33.5 wonderful years of marriage. God made a way providing strength in battling spousal cancer a second time when breast cancer invaded my loving second wife and even a third time after eight years of her cancer being in remission. God made a way for living life despite tough financial market loss experienced immediately upon retirement. God made a way and continues to make a way living under limited income in retirement.

It is hoped this book is inspiring someone else to accept the life given to them; to recognize the importance of personal motivation and dedicate themselves to pressing forward to accept satisfaction in gaining the most from within the resources available to them. Yes, the words of Philippians 4:11 have taught me contentment, accepting who I am, living within the resources that I have, and accepting whatever situation I am living in knowing "God Will Make A Way!"

May this story add strength to the necessary family values needed to guide a young child; add strength to the thought process included in parents allowing heroic dreams of young children to develop personal values; add strength to the importance of guided peer interaction leading to exploring and finding teenage values; and provide encouragement to include discipline, love, and support in exhibiting God-fearing values within each home.

May this book provide perspective and priority so that we will not be fooled into believing that simply accepting the simple faith that God is real will provide a life filled with fame, fortune, and happiness, but is a plan for our lives to make positive changes, turn from living selfishly in hopes of gaining worldly pleasures, and recognize the need to use all the Godly resources available to reap the benefits of living a life of faith.

I have learned God is real! I have learned to allow

God's love to shower me with the blessings available when living in obedience to God's principles and aggressively pressing forward to the prize of His high calling as directed in Philippians 3:14: "I press toward the mark for the prize of the high calling of God in Christ Jesus."

I have learned where my strength comes from in times of trouble, and I have learned to accept each setback as an opportunity to learn how better to face the next adversity. I have learned that through my weaknesses, God has made me strong to face whatever life brings in the future. I like and claim as my guide the holy Scripture of 1 John 5:4: "For whatsoever is born of God overcometh the world; and this is the victory that overcometh the world, even our faith."

Yes, I have learned that God will make a way … no matter what!

Wow!

Chapter 16
#Jesus... Retirement

What does trusting God have to do with how much money it will take to live in retirement? How do you know if you have enough money to start retirement? How do you measure if a person is successful in retirement? How do you plan for a happy retirement?

Retirement is something that we always hear we should be planning for even at an early age. The reality is, however, retirement seems so many years away in the eyes of a young adolescent that it is often not taken seriously until life suddenly lifts us into an age that conventional ways of preparing for retirement become very difficult and stressful.

A person starting his career in the workplace is normally given the option of including a portion of their paycheck towards retirement but very few have the vision that their decision is going to greatly impact their future retirement. It appears so far away to a person starting not only his or her first job, but maybe starting his or her marriage, his or her family, his or her home, or experiencing life on his or her own for the first time. Retirement will happen someday, but making it a priority in the early stages of life seems unimportant.

Experience tells me that retirement planning for a young new worker is easier than for someone who has been in the workforce for twenty years because the amount of "available extra money" is greater. It is the vision of retirement that is not comprehended early in our work lives, and retirement often gets pushed behind the immediate personal financial wants and needs that affect our daily lifestyle.

Reality for me was making ends meet financially and including just a small portion for retirement after making sure immediate family needs were met from paycheck to paycheck. Although good financial planning is offered even in today's workplace, retirement savings and preparation are rarely high on the priority list in the early years of employment.

How then do those who live to retirement age make it? My story is personal but may be helpful for anyone looking to achieve a comfortable retirement lifestyle.

When I had my first job, I thought that if I worked hard everyday, I would earn wages that would be rewarded annually with a pay raise and if I controlled the amount of debt necessary to raise a family and paid all my bills on time, the end result would be a happy retirement.

The problem with that approach is that "everything depended on my performance": my life decisions, my wants and desires in life, my plans, and my way of thinking. I did not keep in mind three things as I planned for my retirement: (1) my boss was in control of my raises; (2) nature was in control of my family's future needs; (3) I could not control the economic conditions of the world (the market) that would affect my family in the future.

The reality was, I could only offer myself, and I learned quickly the outcome was always totally in the hands of someone else guiding my life along the way. I had to put my trust in the many different employers who steered my work life, paid me a fair wage, and offered a retirement that would help put away funds for the future. Early in my working career, an insurance salesman convinced me of how to protect my family financially in case I died with one of those term policies that could easily flip to a "whole life" benefit. It seemed as wages increased, financial planners knocked on the door and it appeared everyone was making sure I was on target to have enough money to one day retire without any worries or unnecessary concerns.

The end result may surprise you! Retirement is wonderful and I have become one of the richest men in the world!

Please understand "one of the richest men in the world" is not a phrase reflecting money, but a statement of contentment, satisfaction, joy, peace, and happiness. All those guidelines I learned along the way, proved extremely helpful in meeting basic family needs. Something happened, though, that was not talked about by employers, financial planners, insurance salespeople, or retirement experts; it involved taking all that good information, all the financial gain, all the life experiences, and letting go of the personal control. Yes, I learned that letting go of my personal control and trusting God to lead my retirement was the advice no one gave in the corporate financial planning world.

I learned in Psalm 37:5: "Commit thy way unto the Lord; trust also in him; and he shall bring it to pass." Psalm 118:8 says, "It is better to trust in the Lord than to put confidence in man." Proverbs 3:5 has become a daily challenge to "trust in the Lord with all thine heart; and lean not unto thine own understanding."

The best plans had truly failed. I worked hard throughout life. I was rewarded financially and had built a retirement account that promised a normal comfortable retirement. However, open heart surgery, retirement three years earlier than anticipated, a world financial market that dropped dramatically, and a wonderful employer watching as promised high value stock options disappeared, all occurred within six months after retirement. It is estimated my financial retirement portfolio lost $600K when the stock market fell from $55 a share to only $1 a share, forcing me to lose all my value in bank stock options that could no longer be exercised or cashed in for profit. All the hard work that earned incentive stock options over the years of successful employment were all lost and it was totally out of my control.

Despite it all, life is comfortable, needs are being met, and the future is exciting!

The difference is, despite a lack of growth in my financial portfolio due to circumstances out of my control (much like my career was being controlled by someone else), my lifestyle remains high quality because, along the journey, I discovered to "let go" of my choices for financial direction and to follow the principles of living a life spent serving and giving to God. I have seen the truth of Matthew 6:19-20 come alive in my personal life, despite personal losses, in trusting the biblical Word: "Lay not up for yourselves treasures upon earth, where moth and rust doth corrupt, and where thieves break through and steal; But lay up for yourselves treasures in heaven, where neither moth nor rust doth corrupt, and where thieves do not break through nor steal."

Yes, I learned the principle of serving and giving to God. Just as I trusted employers, world financial experts, insurance salespeople and banking professionals, I have placed everything in the hands of my Lord and Savior Jesus Christ. I have learned that giving a portion of my income to God every Sunday as a love offering has provided personal returns of provisions that only a faithful God can deliver.

Learning from Mom and Dad the importance of giving my life to Jesus at a young age of twelve, and committing to live more like Jesus at age twenty-one, were the two elements that no one could change or take away from me. With God in my life, this sustained my retirement when all the high performing assets managers started scrambling to cover losses in the financial downfall that began in 2006.

My retirement claim of being "one of the richest men in the world" comes from trusting God and allowing Him to use all the skills learned in the working world as driving forces in my life today. Satisfaction and contentment are highlighted in the joy I now experience as my play-by-play radio experience was key in accepting an invitation to be the public address announcer voice of the men's and women's basketball at Auburn University Montgomery. My banking career allowed me the honor of serving on the first ever MAX Credit Union Leasing Operations Committee. My law enforcement background allowed me the privilege of serving in retirement as president of Central Alabama Crimestoppers.

My community leadership developed in my working career got me invited to help develop a City Crime Free Weekend. My love for teaching in church during a busy working career led me to serving in retirement weekly with the homeless and street friends of west side Montgomery and within my retirement church. Mission trips to Chile, the Dominican Republic, India, and New Orleans, and doing mission work with tornado disaster relief teams with the Alabama Baptist Association, have filled my heart seeing how obedient faith in God truly works.

Living in a comfortable home with fishing lakes

nearby and an exercise pool in the backyard is what I describe as a piece of Heaven on earth. Watching God accept our offerings and in return providing our daily needs is overwhelming. God delivered on His promise in Matthew 6:33 saying, "But seek ye first the kingdom of God, and his righteousness; and all these things shall be added unto you."

What is the secret to having enough to enjoy at retirement?

Take advantage of those early retirement savings opportunities, work hard, give your body to your employer but your heart, soul, and mind to God. He will never leave you, nor forsake you (Hebrews 13:5). He will supply all your needs (Philippians 4:19). He will be your shield and your strength (Isaiah 41:10). Yes, trusting God pays dividends forever!

Store up your treasures in Heaven and He will fill your barns to overflowing (Proverbs 3:10). Yes, I believe the biblical words of Matthew 6:31-32: "Therefore take no thought, saying, What shall we eat? or What shall we drink? or Wherewithal shall we be clothed? For your heavenly Father knoweth that ye have need of all these things."

Am I truly one of the richest men in the world? I think so; but you can move ahead of me if you so desire. That is up to you! You can do better and become that person if you choose. Do it for your family. It will be a retirement that will become, as a popular TV commercial says, "priceless!"

I claim for you the Bible verse, Proverbs 10:22: "The blessing of the Lord, it maketh rich, and he addeth no sorrow to it."

CHAPTER 17
#Jesus... Simply Trust

How do you know when trusting God is working? That is a question that if one could answer would launch a significant event so powerful that change in the world would happen unknowingly from within the hearts and minds of individuals.

It is also a question that can only be answered as events become reality following completion and settlement of their resolution.

I can without a doubt say that trusting God works because anyone can look at my life and see that God blessed me, a little boy from Indiana far beyond any expectations of his hard working, God-loving parents from the farm, to the city, to the U.S. Navy, to the schools of hard knocks in the job market, continuing education studies at Indiana University, Colorado University, Ball State University, University of Georgia, and Notre Dame, to church and community voluntary leadership, to the foreign mission fields of Chile, the Dominican Republic and India, to the local mission field in West Montgomery and into retirement in a suburb community called Pike Road in "Sweet Home Alabama."

How do you know when trusting God is working? Discovering that answer often times cannot be seen visibly but requires faith, believing in a spiritual God who created this great land and who reigns over Heaven and earth. Hebrews 11:6 has taught me the following: "But without faith it is impossible to please him; for he that cometh to God must believe that he is, and that he is a rewarder of them that diligently seek him." I have been motivated also by Ephesians 6:6: "Not with eyeservice, as menpleasers; but as the servants of Christ, doing the will of God from the heart." I have found strength in James 1:6: "But let him ask in faith, nothing wavering. For he that wavereth is like a wave of the sea driven with the wind and tossed."

Yes, I have discovered I am blessed by the same all-powerful God who: formed man from the elements of the earth (Genesis 1); created woman from a rib of man (Genesis 2:21-22); told Noah to build an ark in the middle of a drought (Genesis 5:13-14); erased earth of its people in the Great Flood; replenished all with a rainbow of promise (Genesis 9:13); directed Abraham to "get thee out of thy country" and promised to "make of thee a great nation, and I will bless thee, and make thy name great," (Genesis 12:1-2). The same God that after total commitment of the father raising a knife to kill his son, Isaac, in obedience, provided a sacrifice saving the young boy (Genesis 22:9-13). The same God who sent His Son, Jesus, to be born of a virgin and placed in a manager (Luke 1:27- Luke 2:7); walk this earth as any other man, but with perfection voluntarily leading to a horrendous crucifixion on a cross all for the love and salvation of you and me (Luke 2:42 thru Luke 23:56). The same God who after being dead for three days and buried in a stone-protected grave, raised His crucified Son, Jesus, from the tomb with a resurrection miracle assuring everyone who believes of having eternal life hereafter with Him (Luke 24:1-53)!

Living the pains of daily life often blurs our vision, but it is the perfect 20/20 hindsight that only experience can teach in understanding and recognizing the blessings that get us through one situation at a time.

Hindsight reveals clear thinking on the other side of circumstances and points to a decisive means higher than our own at bringing its conclusion. Not all results are what we were striving to accomplish, but each proves the best for our personal growth.

Trust does not always return our choice of favorable outcome, but I have learned without a doubt it is the best avenue for success.

God honors those who honor Him and there is no better way to bring glory to His name than by trusting!

I discovered that fame and fortune are not guaranteed; but I am pleased to admit that trusting the Word of God has delivered personal satisfaction and peace in my heart!

I choose to trust in God!

Chapter 18
#Jesus...
Barrel Life, Good Example

A prime example of trusting in God can be seen in the Church at the Barrel located in west Montgomery, Alabama, where four and a half years of experience serving the under-privileged is reflected in personal behavior changes that are positively affecting the environment of a neighborhood of homeless and street people.

When discovered by Jeff and Trudy McFarland, missionaries of Urban TREC and TREC International, the area of Rosa Parks & Stone Streets was like any other neglected area of west Montgomery where landlords offer the poorest of houses to the homeless and street living population. About five guys were often seen standing, weaving, and bobbing around an old fire barrel in the middle of a fenced side yard exchanging stories while filling their bodies with liquid spirits from a cup or bottle, and oftentimes were broken up after a heated exchange of words or actions showing anger and frustration.

Jeff and Trudy began to befriend the men, offering them food and conversation around the barrel. That opened an avenue of trust that has led to an unbelievable outcome four and a half years later. Transformation has occurred in that side yard and men who once lifted the spirit in drink, now lift up spiritual praises to God that is making a difference in the neighborhood.

This chapter will trace some of that journey in an attempt to help readers discover that God loves everyone with the same passion as displayed in His creation, His birth of Jesus, the Crucifixion and the Resurrection, and releases the same Holy Spirit's power in lives today.

Jeff and Trudy trusted God to provide the help in feeding the homeless in that side yard making a commitment to seek His Will in service to the homeless and street folk of the Rosa Parks-Stone Streets neighborhood. It was a huge trust because Jeff and Trudy had just moved from their home in a comfortable subdivision in the more affluent East Montgomery to purchase an older two-story home directly in the heart of a much poorer neighborhood on the west side where crimes of all sorts were routine occurrences. Their commitment was to help make a positive difference in that tough area. For three years, they held church services in their home and continue today giving food, shelter, and clothing to the less fortunate in that west Montgomery area.

Approached by friends from their former church, Jeff demanded only one condition when offered their unconditional love and support in building relationships around that fire barrel. That condition was that once started, we will not stop, because only a long-term commitment would be effective in reaching and helping our new friends. I was privileged to teach the class of young married couples who were led to help Jeff and Trudy minister to the homeless and street folks.

Trusting God for His provisions, the Life Changing Bible Sunday School Class at Vaughn Forest Baptist Church accepted the call for service to extend love to the homeless and street people of the neighborhood around that west side intersection where many people were suffering with addictions of drugs, alcohol, gambling, prostitution, and other devastating personal situations.

Prayers were lifted for guidance, direction, boldness, protection, and wisdom in launching a meaningful ministry at the barrel. Volunteers pray each week to personally strap on the spiritual armor of Ephesians Chapter 6 before each visit to the barrel neighborhood.

In the beginning, Bible study was delivered while standing around the barrel. It led to sitting on overturned buckets or an old discarded lawn chair as men began to grow in number when the neighborhood suddenly noticed something special was happening down at 512 Stone Street. The five men grew to ten, then fifteen, and today an audience of twenty-five to fifty people are gathered at noon on each Tuesday.

The many names of the individuals attending at one time or another have reached more than 500 in that side yard. The neighborhood has over 200 meals served on each Thanksgiving service held outside at that intersection. One of the original men standing around the barrel said he came to receive the "bird with the Word" and that phrase remains the call to service around that fiery barrel today. It has become known as attending the Church at the Barrel each Tuesday as the "bird with the Word" is offered with a Bible study taught followed by the serving of fried chicken.

The scene is a side yard between a house known for

neighborhood pleasures of multiple addictions and a rental house where street folk gathered. Stumps have been cut from trees by Bobby Coon of that original Sunday School Class and used for seating for sixty people. A wood fence built by volunteers and two crosses placed at the corners of the yard creates an outdoor amphitheater for discussions. An old picnic table has become the center point for the food serving line.

Jeff and Trudy follow a format of meeting noon to 1 p.m. each Tuesday with a time of greeting each other, sometimes singing of praise music, Bible study, and the serving of fried chicken, two slices of bread, a small bag of potato chips, a Rice Krispies treat, a napkin, and a bottle of water. Sometimes cookies and other snacks would be brought by loving volunteers. The results of trusting God are so apparent in that format because only fifty pieces of chicken are ordered each week, but if fifteen show up or as many as fifty-five, the food table never runs out even though each person being fed is able to get back in line to receive as many as three pieces of chicken. It compares to the biblical story of God increasing the five loaves of bread and only two fish to feed the 5,000 as described in the Bible in Mark 6:38-44. It happens each week!

God has blessed the efforts of the Church at the

Barrel from their humble beginnings when outbursts (sometimes violent) were normal as Jeff would be teaching, compared to today, when quiet, attentive friends sit studying together giving positive feedback and offering spiritual conversation. In the beginning, the yard was fenced and entrance was gained through a gate that was normally locked except on Tuesdays. The home adjacent to the yard was in poor condition with gaping holes in sections of the structure, no electricity or water, but it was occupied by one of the men who was always around the barrel. One rainy day everyone was forced inside from the wetness only to have the floor collapse when everyone rushed around the same spot of the room reaching for the "chicken bucket." As is often the case, the tenant man had to disappear for lack of meeting the required monthly payment to his landlord. God made a way for Jeff to rent the house at a reduced price and Urban TREC became lessee in the "hood."

Trusting God has fed and taught Bible study in that homeless neighborhood at noon each Tuesday since February 2010 through provisions provided by volunteers serving weekly, supporters of many church Sunday School classes donating money for food, and the every week cooking of the chicken by a "deli crew" at Chantilly Wal-Mart in East Montgomery. God has multiplied the personal resources in unbelievable ways so much so that the chicken box never runs empty until each homeless or street friend has been fed and the food line is empty!

Support for the Church at the Barrel comes from as far away as Indiana as God-loving individuals each donate $1 a week to purchase the necessary food provisions. Visitors have come from India, South Africa, England, Switzerland, and many from the United States. One special guest sitting on the stumps and helping teach in the now renovated rental house included a NBA champion and a celebrity basketball analyst. Volunteers include: teachers, retired military personnel, lawyers, bankers, missionaries, housewives, college students, businessmen, retired coaches, and many married couples with their families.

Miracles have happened at the Barrel! Isaac, who said he has been drunk everyday since 1993, was within minutes of life-support being turned off in a hospital ICU, when praying brothers at the Barrel called upon God to heal his body. Issac received his miracle healing and months later returned to the Barrel to encourage others to look at what God had done for him! Isaac went into total rehab at a nearby VA Center and moved into a home with a sister. He often can be found visiting the west side neighborhood.

Henry overcame his dependency on alcohol addiction, was baptized after accepting Jesus as Lord and Savior, and was invited by a daughter to come off the streets and live in her home in the state of New York.

Loraine would sit afternoons under the influence in a side yard next door to the Barrel. She would watch the weekly "bird with the Word" sessions through a wire fence until, one day, she accepted a homeless friend's invitation to come participate. Her decision resulted in a renewed will to follow Jesus and to be baptized. Two weeks later, it was learned she had acted upon her new strength and moved into an apartment in a senior housing area.

Bobby came to the Barrel every week, prayed for work, and was given a second chance by an apartment construction crew and when his work term was finished, he had re-developed labor and work ethic skills that has him consistently working handyman jobs today.

Sheila tells the story of how an unknown man appeared and approached her while she was standing late one night ready to jump off a bridge railing into the flowing river beneath. All the man said was, "God does not want you to do that," and she stepped down to safety. Sheila accepted the love of Jesus and followed in believer's baptism. She faithfully comes to the Barrel each week praising God for her renewed life.

Rodney was a quiet homeless man who was always in attendance at the Barrel and very thankful for a warm coat, a new pair of socks, or an occasional ride. He was like a bigger protective brother who said very little but whose actions were noticed by everyone. He accepted Jesus in his heart at the Barrel. Little did anyone know that just months later, Rodney would die unexpectedly. Friends found joy knowing Rodney would no longer be cold, hungry, or lonely as God lovingly accepted his soul in eternal Heaven. It was another miracle performed at the Barrel.

Not everyone accepts the life of Christ at the Barrel, but all are impacted. Ask big Ernest! He was prayed over following a "ball bat beating from an alleged loan shark" and given assistance at regaining his life. He has been helped on numerous attempts to get off the streets, but continues to fall victim to addiction and, therefore, still struggles with survival. Many, however, of the homeless and street men and women who come to the Barrel struggle everyday to overcome their addictions and have discovered that "trusting God" has awakened a new desire to get up everyday, restored hope in their personal value/esteem system, and provided an understanding that through all the heartache and hard times, God has a purpose for them to live another day.

Ben is a young man who has been placed in rehabilitation three times, and although he completed a required one full year in his last attempt, he continues to struggle. Despite having the sharp ability to work and take care of himself, he will not "leave" the addictive neighborhood lifestyle. Ben is often the one helping others and keeping peace in the yard, but despite his good qualities, he battles the demons of alcohol everyday. He is again looking and asking for a fourth chance at restoration.

Their trust is being rewarded with job opportunities in the same neighborhood at the Barrel site. Volunteers who serve each week can see the lifestyle improvements that are happening in the once forgotten neighborhood that became a collection point for homeless and street life addictions of drugs, alcohol, gambling, prostitution and who knows what else! Apparently the city of Montgomery is also witnessing the "turnaround" because they have approved a business incubator owner to build a site down the street that is described as the first step to seeing job creation and renewal of positive life in an area blighted by abandoned old buildings.

Volunteers credit the obedience of men and women

who have made spiritual commitments to change their personal lifestyles while attending the outdoor Church at the Barrel as being rewarded by God for their faithfulness.

The new business employer announced plans to hopefully hire applicants from the neighborhood to launch the first phase of the business incubator... Wow, Trusting God works!

Our homeless and street friends are being restored by their personal faith to regain their sense of worth to others and the community, rebuilding their self-esteem, developing renewed confidence, and finding a burning desire in their hearts to use their workable skills and talents once again.

It brings pure joy and satisfaction to see an awakening in our homeless and street friends from the Church at the Barrel that makes them want to start each new day choosing to meet whatever challenges might come their way.

Trusting God is producing lifestyle changes at the Barrel that can be seen through God's Word in Hebrews 11:1, which states, "Now faith is the substance of things hoped for, the evidence of things not seen." Yes, Jeff and Trudy did not just see lost lonely men staggering back and forth at 512 Stone

Street back in 2010; they believed with spiritual faith the five men would one day be transformed into useful, loving friends through the power of the living God. That faith and vision is producing positive results in that neighborhood.

In four years, an old neglected home and side yard have been transformed from a neighborhood of homeless men swinging to natural spirits of alcohol and drugs, to a standing on a piece of ground volunteers compared to the "holy ground" described when God spoke to Moses in the Old Testament in Genesis chapter 3. It is now changed into a place where all who come are having their hearts lifted by the Spirit of God. Yes, serving the "bird with the Word" is a great example of trusting God through serving a combination of physical and spiritual food every Tuesday between noon and 1 p.m.

It is truly amazing how trusting God has brought together men and women so drastically different from the east side and west side of Montgomery who find personal satisfaction serving alongside each other.

Wow… Trusting God works!

Chapter 19
#Jesus...
The First Shall Be Last

Trusting God has given me a life that makes me wish that somehow the last chapter of my life could have been the first chapter of my life.

Isn't it something when you realize it took all your life just to learn how wonderful it is to simply enjoy the journey? Why do we press so hard and struggle so long attempting to "get it all right" before we can relax in retirement?

As a child, I am sure I was grabbing at my bottle or my clothes instead of relaxing and allowing family to freely nurture and care for me.

As a middle school student, I am sure I was aggressive at trying to outdo my friends and to show them my way was better, or my things were more important, while learning how to "one-up" others instead of discovering new ways to enjoy each personality and lifestyle while growing.

As a teenager, I am sure I had all the answers when it came to deciding what was best for me instead of listening and accepting the guidance my loving parents exhibited from their dedicated lifetime of experience. I remember a moment that is now embarrassing for me but at the time probably seemed very naïve to my dad. It was the night before I left for my first day in the Navy, and my dad was giving me some last minute advice. He asked me why I was joining the Navy and most likely was hoping I might give some wonderful patriotic answer to proudly share later with Mom. However, being the smart child that I thought I was, in my youthful mind I simply said, "Dad, I am going because I am tired of the people of Greensburg telling me what to do with my life!" My loving father did not say a word, but I am sure as soon as I disappeared from that father-son talk, he broke out in laughter knowing that as of 0800 (Navy time) the next day, I would have everyone in the military giving me orders and taking control of my life until completion and discharge from service. Dad must have thought, "Yes, my son, Bob, has a lot to learn and I can't wait to see how Uncle Sam shapes his life!"

As an adult, I'm sure I thought my ideas and my

desires were superior to the advice that any mentor, aged co-worker, peer, or supervisor gave me, instead of considering the best team approach or end result to solutions, or how others were affected by my decisions.

As a retired person, I am now sure that I could not have succeeded in this "last chapter" of my life without the unrecognized love, guidance, nurturing, discipline, and prayer of so many others along the way. I am happy to claim Proverbs 22:6: "Train up a child in the way he should go; and when he is old, he will not depart from it." Thank you, Mom and Dad!

Isn't it ironic? Somehow I made it only to find that now there is very little time left to share the valuable lessons learned with a world that is spinning so fast no one has time to listen.

Now, I understand and can relate to a convicted felon in Bullock County Prison near Union Springs, Alabama. Participating with a prison ministry team from Vaughn Forest Church of Montgomery, we had just finished an inspirational worship service where an estimated 150 prison inmates came to the chapel altar signing a "Courageous Resolution" claiming a desire to change their lives, declaring a will to take responsibility seriously, to love and honor their families, to forgive and reconcile, to treat others with kindness, and to actively turn from their past life to seeking God's strength to courageously walk in obedience to His commands.

It was on the exit walk along the prison hallway afterward when an inmate broke my silent thoughts with an excited, profound statement: "Isn't it something? I had to come to prison for twenty years to find Jesus… and you know, I am glad I did because I found Him tonight!" He then turned right abruptly and disappeared into his over-crowded, noisy cell block giving a wave of friendship and compassion as our team headed out into the free world to return home.

If only the "last chapter of our life" could have been the "first chapter!" I am sure we would all do things differently!

Wow! I know trusting God early in life would have motivated me to honor my earthly father and mother even more, to respect without hesitation my family members and friends, to show more unconditional love to my wife and children each day of my life, and to give 100-percent effort to all my employers and mentors. I know I would have followed Jesus with commitment rather than attempting to lead asking for continual prayers to clear my path. Good news: You still have time to get your "chapters" in order!

CHAPTER 20
#Jesus... Gifts From God

Children are truly a gift from God and they also are, perhaps, one of the greatest examples of proof that God is real and also proof that trusting God is essential and rewarding!

Our family has its share of examples.

It seems like yesterday when our oldest daughter, Kimberly Ann, was given some bad news. I came home from work to find Kim, now married and happily settled in a house with her husband, Bob, visiting. I could see her outside the kitchen furiously shooting basketball in the backyard. After asking my wife what she was doing, I learned Kim's doctor told her they could not find the developing baby's heartbeat and could only see a "blob" during her first trimester. In addition to that, they told her to go home and get rid of the baby.

I was shocked and I immediately went running

outside, shouting for Kim to come in the house where we claimed that only God could give authority over life and death. We prayed for a miracle.

To God be the glory! That baby that she was told had no life and and to get rid of, has now graduated from Auburn University and has completed his second of three years of Jones School of Law at Faulkner University where he is studying to be an attorney in Montgomery, AL. Yes, Jason Herbert is full of life and this summer will marry the southern belle of his eye. He is a living testimony that God is real and worth trusting! God continued to bless Kim's obedient life and she and Bob also gave birth to Joshua, who at this writing is entering his junior year in college. Then the Lord blessed them with Jacob, a graduating high school senior who already has enlisted in the Air National Guard to serve his country.

Other tests of trusting God were seen in our Debbie when she had three miscarriages before God blessed her life with the births of three little boys: Zachary, today a high school senior about to graduate who along the path has already performed on the professional ballet stage; Jackson, who has developed beyond early childhood struggles to enjoy high school academic and social skills that have given him satisfaction and high grades; and brother, McKay, who participates in three sports and is moving into his freshman year, attesting that faith in God and obedient living will produce miracles in one's life.

Our son, Matthew, saw his mother die of cancer while he was a sophomore in college, but his zeal to press forward (Philippians 3:14) took him to the mission fields in the Philippines and China and launched a career that has his life totally dependent upon the ministry of serving others through his love for God. His "Shoot for Life" ministry provides financial help and spiritual hope to cancer treatment patients and provides encouragement and strength for couples to trust and follow God in their quest for happiness and satisfaction. God has blessed Matthew and Andrea with six children; three girls: Alea, Olivea, and Emelea; and three boys: Trey, Colt, and baby Knox!

Matthew, our third child, was born following a family decision to sponsor a little boy in Haiti. Eight years had passed from the birth of our two earlier Bostic baby girls, and everyone thought God had completed the Bostic family. Within a few months of excitedly sponsoring that little Haitian boy named Caleb Lucian, my wife was unexpectedly pregnant and our son, Matthew, was born two days before Christmas. Matthew's name came from a dream his mother had in her final trimester of pregnancy. She related to us how that God showed her the face of her unborn son and she knew in her heart our boy was a gift from God. She knew that night his name would be Matthew meaning, "Gift of God!" We learned later our Haitian boy, Caleb, grew up to become a pastor in his native land.

One of the hardest miracles was experienced upon the death of Kimberly, Deborah, and Matthew's mother, Joanie. God healed their mother of the horrible disease of cancer when He called her home to Heaven on April 27, 1995, ending a short battle of eight months and two days after doctors diagnosed her with an incurable rare form of leukemia that doctors said caused a chromosome switch in her body at age fifty-one. The miracle was the inspiration it planted in each child to live life loving their families each day going forward with the realization that every day is a blessing and we are to live it to its fullest, knowing that God is real and only in trusting Him can one overcome the daily challenges and reach satisfaction.

Their life was cut short of enjoying their mother for a few more days, but they experienced God's love for her when He ended her suffering and opened the pearly gates of Heaven to a life without anymore pain to live eternally, walking those paved streets of gold in heavenly peace and joy! Death was sad and heartbreaking, but knowing the gift of eternal life with Jesus was delivered to their mother at her untimely death was truly life changing!

The miracles continued as sons, Jason and Jared, became brothers in the Bostic family. Following the death of my Joanie, God laid upon my heart the needs of two young boys being raised by their mother. Inquiring into their lives started a casual acquaintance around a youth baseball diamond that led to God healing a broken heart (mine) and returning love to a dedicated and committed Christian lady (Melissa) and a marriage that all the children endorsed and encouraged.

The prayers of friends praying for two individuals (me and Melissa) in separate prayer chains were answered, culminating in a marriage that brought comfort, peace, healing, joy, and love to the two of us. It was the uniting of two families from the depths of heartache that was totally out of anyone's control but God Almighty's!

God's promise in Matthew 6:33 to "seek God first in our lives and all these things will be added unto you" came alive to Melissa and me. Seeking God first provided a peace that passes all understanding (Philippians 4:7), and it also showed God delivering two adults out of sadness and loneliness into a purpose-filled life as God bound two hurting families into one.

Only God can over-rule a husband who prayed for love to be taken away from his heart after losing his high school sweetheart to cancer. Only God can refill the heart of a God-serving woman with love lost when forced to raise two children alone. Only God can hear the prayers of a people calling for new life for their suffering friends, and only God can provide the witness of a family made whole from situations deemed devastating. Indeed, God was in control! Trusting God, for me, made the impossible possible as love was rekindled in my broken heart. I truly believe the verse in Matthew 19:26: "With men this is impossible; but with God all things are possible!"

It was evident that God was blessing our families as the court system permitted a speedy adoption of Jason and Jared to become Bostic boys and our new life was launched bringing the new Bostic household to five children dedicated to moving forward with Christian convictions.

Jason had graduated from college and was teaching when a miscarriage saddened their young marriage only to be reversed into healing that saw God bless him and his wife, Michelle, with two more children — a son, Ethan, and a daughter, Emmelyne. God rewarded them for their faith in Him. Only God can hear the prayers and see the effort of a young teenager working to help his mother support the household, give him a new family, give him a name and a life of encouragement, and see him advance from early restaurant service employment into a position of principal administration in a highly respected school district near Birmingham.

Son, Jared, watched his southern belle bride, Rachel, develop a medical condition called ulcerative colitis. When she became pregnant they battled constant trips to the hospital for treatment and care. It became so severe that Rachel experienced intestinal blockages and had to undergo two surgeries during her second trimester of pregnancy and became very high risk for a successful birth forcing continual monitoring of the baby. Rachel had to surgically have a wound vac attached and was put on a feeding procedure that included being fed intravenously for the final 100 days of her pregnancy.

Although the delivery date was set for November 1, 2011, complications forced hospital admission on September 23rd. Doctors, fighting to save both baby and mamma, decided on September 27th, while Rachel was under heavy medication for pain and nausea, to move quickly, and with the help of an additional top notch general surgeon in the operating room standing next to the baby's doctor, to prematurely deliver the beautiful little boy named Levi Andrew Bostic at 9:01 a.m., weighing 6 lbs 9 oz and 19 inches long.

Born early at thirty-five weeks with underdeveloped lungs, Levi was gasping for air with what doctors described as "wet lungs" and immediately contracted pneumonia. Trusting God was never more important than in the next twenty-three days when those precious nurses (angels) of the NICU wing of Baptist East Hospital in Montgomery, AL, constantly loved, stroked, and administered needle pricks to his developing spine. They constantly ran medical tests, gave x-ray scans, and nursed our thirteenth grandchild. He slowly advanced from a feeding tube to the bottle, and was eventually sent home after three weeks and two days. Hallelujah! God has now completely healed both Levi and his mother, and their family has been fully blessed with a healthy son now approaching three years of age.

I never understood why God put Melissa and me together until nine months into our new marriage. Melissa was diagnosed with breast cancer and had to undergo surgery and take the necessary, but very tough chemotherapy and radiation treatments over the next several months. Little did we know that although God healed Melissa's body, she would eight years later be stricken a second time with breast cancer on the other side of her body that again required surgery and those dreaded chemo and radiation treatments and with all the personal side effects. Little did I know that God would graciously put me at her side to help and support her during that difficult time in her life.

God wanted me to learn through supporting Joanie in her incurable battle with cancer that life doesn't always deliver us what we desire. It was at the grave that I accepted His spiritual lesson that life is intended to be lived unto the Lord realizing that one day we will all die and our bodies will return to the soil from which it came. I committed on that burial day to continue to live serving Jesus in any way I could in honor of the love He had shown the Bostic family.

As the words to the song "God Will Make a Way" rang loud and clear in my mind, I was reminded once again that God was in control.

Yes, God is real!

Miracles have been threaded throughout the Bostic family and the only explanation is a foundation rooted by parents who lived and taught by example and passed on to me the normal everyday life of loving each other, helping others, working hard with integrity, and trusting God to provide all our needs (Philippians 4:19). Passing it on to our children was only natural!

Hopefully you will be inspired to do the same!

Wow…. Trusting God works!

Chapter 21
#Jesus...
27 Reasons To Trust

I have twenty-seven immediate reasons to know trusting God works!

I see it at each full family visit in our home. I see it at each activity I attend for my grandchildren. And I see it in five wholesome families enjoying each other in love, respect, and honor in the living rooms of our children.

I remember proudly how that number was higher counting when Mom and Dad sacrificed for me. I recall my four brothers inspiring me to follow them as they blazed the life trail ahead of me.

I will never forget the love of Joanie, and I cherish the many prayers her mother, Mammaw Myrtle, lifted for us. God has sent many wonderful friends my way—friends who gave me true reason to trust God.

And I know the many wonderful friends God has led into my life pushed my true reasons for trusting to perhaps as many as the heavenly stars shining each night. And, believe it or not, I should also count my special friend, Gracie, a rescued puppy that is the best lap dog companion in the world.

Yes, the count is currently twenty-seven family members, but will be twenty-eight when my first grandchild, Jason, marries sweet Sydney in a few weeks, and on and on the blessings pour. I am so reminded of Malachi 3:10 when God said if we "bring our tithes into the storehouse, I will open you the windows of heaven and pour you out a blessing that there shall not be room enough to receive it."

My cup runs over with love, joy, peace, long suffering, kindness, goodness, faithfulness, gentleness, and self-control as described in the Holy Scripture as the fruits of the Spirit found in Galatians 5:22.

Wow… God is real and trusting God is the best advice anyone can share with a friend!

Here are my 27 reasons for trusting God:

Kimberly & Bob Herbert and sons: Jason, Josh, and Jacob. (Sydney becomes Jason's bride this summer.)

Deborah & Scott Taylor and sons: Zachary, Jackson, and McKay.

Matthew & Andrea Bostic and daughters: Alea, Olivea, and Emelea; and sons: Trey, Colt, and Knox.

Jason & Michelle Bostic and son, Ethan, and daughter, Emmelyne.

Jared and Rachel Bostic and son, Levi.

Proud parents, Bob & Melissa Bostic!

Wow…my Joanie perhaps said it best when she would always smile and sing the chorus "God Is So Good!"

#Jesus… Wow… Trusting God Works!

Chapter 22
#Jesus...
Steps to Trusting God

Now that you have read my story of how trusting God has provided me a life into retirement that gives personal satisfaction and joy beyond normal measures of wealth and personal possessions, I am inspired to suggest helpful steps that you might implement into your own lifestyle.

I hope to write a second edition of #Jesus and discuss specific steps in detail but want to share at this time enough information to help anyone begin the personal process towards achieving the abundant life that I so often referred to throughout this book.

Just like that simple but now famous list, printed in Author Ron Clark's book, "THE ESSENTIAL 55," gave rules that adults should teach children to be accountable for in achieving a successful life, my experience points to a simple but important strategy of steps that will enable readers to trust God for all things. I am so reminded of Matthew 6:33 when Jesus says "seek ye first the kingdom of God, and his righteousness; and all these things shall be added unto you."

I have discovered it was these specific steps that proved key to my satisfied life:

Believe:	Believe in the God of the universe who not only created this great world but who loves you so much that He sent His Son, Jesus, to die for you and me, providing a way for us to have eternal life in heaven.
Relationship:	Seek God as Lord and Savior, developing a personal relationship that He will honor by placing His Holy Spirit in your heart.
Commitment:	Commit to live more like Christ everyday.
Priorities:	Make pleasing God your motivator in all that you do.
Prayer:	Include personal time to pray with God everyday.
Lead:	Follow God then lead others.
Study:	Prepare for each day's challenges through study of God's word.
Plan:	Find direction by planning strategies to achieve life's goals.
Accountability:	Chose someone to question and hold you accountable for actions.

Measure:	Evaluate your progress to stay on course.
Adjust:	Be willing to correct a wrong turn.
Flexibility:	Leave room for constructive criticism.
Persevere:	Never stop or give up living for or like Jesus.
Celebrate:	Personal victories and blessings warrant celebration.
Obedience:	God will bless your obedience for following him.
Faith:	Stand strong even when you can not see beyond the storm.
Focus:	Keep your eyes on Jesus through all circumstances.
Share:	Tell others about Jesus and what He has done in your life.

#Jesus...
Stay Connected

Writing this book has been a labor of love for me and it has inspired a vision to stay connected with readers offering hope and encouragement to trust God while living and progressing through life's journey.

The many forms of communications now available worldwide actually makes it very easy and convenient and it is my hope you will consider an option to keep in touch in the future. I have plans to continue sharing how God is blessing and guiding my life and I plan to share lessons I learn with others who might be attempting to find reason and purpose in their similar journeys in life.

I am posting addresses of my email, twitter, and blog accounts, and U.S. mail for the convenience of anyone who might on a particular day need to ask a question or seek encouragement in facing life's daily situations.

I also am looking forward to future #**Jesus** books that will explore and discuss topics emerging from reader's feedback and or suggestions of this edition.

Email:	Robert.bostic@yahoo.com
Twitter:	@BobBostic1
Blog:	bobbostic.blogspot.com
U.S. Mail:	Robert L. Bostic 1040 Ivy Bridge Court Pike Road, Al 36064

#Jesus...
God's Blessings

Grandchildren shown at Jason & Sydney's wedding rehearsal dinner.

Joanie Bostic

Melissa Bostic

www.ingramcontent.com/pod-product-compliance
Lightning Source LLC
LaVergne TN
LVHW051559070426
835507LV00021B/2669